ABOUT THE A

Jon Dunckley is a seasoned consultant, engaging speaker, skilled trainer, and accomplished writer. With over 30 years of experience, he proudly identifies as a geek! Despite an impressive educational background that boasts multiple degree-level qualifications across various disciplines, Jon is far from being a dull academic.

As the founding director of About Consulting Group (www.about-consulting.co.uk), he has earned a reputation for simplifying complex concepts to help the people he works with. Everything he does is based around a single mission:

"To help ordinary people achieve extraordinary things."

This goal is what drives him to share his knowledge every day, with as many people as possible. He wants you to have the benefits of his experience in the real world, because it isn't all selfies and sunshine. In fact, Jon will be one of the first to tell you that people who live through a carefully curated social media feed are almost certainly full of crap! Just dig a little deeper, and you'll see they're working through their own challenges with life.

Jon lives in Northampton with his wife, kids, and crazy dogs, which keeps him fairly busy. In what little spare time he has, he competes in triathlons and generally looks for new ways to get into adventures...

First published in 2023.

This book is intended to provide guidance and inspiration. However, it is essential to understand that the author and publisher are not liable for any outcomes or consequences that may arise from the use of the information contained within these pages. The content herein does not constitute a clinical manual, and individual results may vary. It is imperative to consult with a qualified professional if you have any doubts about whether the exercises or advice in this book are suitable for your specific circumstances. By using this book, you accept full responsibility for your actions and decisions.

For my Mum

TABLE OF CONTENTS

REWRITTEN

Changing your internal stories for a
happier and more fulfilled life

JON DUNCKLEY

THE JOURNEY BEGINS...

AS I WRITE this, we're living in challenging times. A war in Europe, a cost-of-living crisis, and global warming that seems to be making the UK colder and wetter whilst burning parts of the Mediterranean to the ground. Yet life isn't all doom and gloom; there are still positives. The key is being willing to rewrite some of the stories you tell yourself so you can see them.

Every day I speak to another person who just feels beaten. Their businesses are struggling, and their home life is taking a hit, because they can't do the things they used to do (and that's after we've survived a pandemic). It's no wonder so many people are feeling low. But, as I listen to the words people say, I'm taken back to who I was in the 1990s. I hear their hopelessness, the belief things can't get better, and that feeling we might as well give up and settle in for a long period of difficulty. Yet, I know there's another way to look at this. I know because I've been there and done it. Let me explain...

The painful realities of graduating

In 1996, I graduated from Leeds University with a Bachelor of Science degree in psychology. Like many students, I'd enjoyed my subject, but was slightly more interested in finding my feet as an adult. I'd attended lectures, read the textbooks, and comfortably passed the exams, but I'd also had a girlfriend, found alcohol, and played quite a lot of pool.

Unfortunately, while life was moving around me, I hadn't taken the time to consider how the content of my psychology lectures might help with the mess which had started to unfold in my own life. As a result, I couldn't stop myself sliding into a catastrophic breakdown that nearly cost me everything.

While I was studying, I'd lost my grandparents, two of the nicest people I've ever known, and a second set of parents to me while growing up. I was struggling with huge debt and a bank manager who seemed intent on shutting off my line of credit. There was nowhere I could call home, and I couldn't seem to find a job, no matter how many doors I knocked. In short, things were grim. I couldn't see a way out. In fact, I was convinced there wasn't one and, I admit, I went to some dark places…until I finally found my way through to the other side.

It took a while for me to see the truth: the power to change everything was already there. I had control of my life, and I could shape it. I could dwell on the knock-backs, or I could remember I was living in one of the wealthiest countries on Earth at the richest time in the planet's history. I had a family who cared for me, and the rest of my life left to achieve the things I wanted to.

It wasn't my life that was bad, it was my perspective.

Of course, I didn't wake up one morning and find everything was suddenly fixed. It certainly wasn't easy to alter my entire mindset (and I'll challenge anyone who tells you to just 'snap out of it'). What I was able to do was see a path to the other side and find steps to help me get there. By concentrating on different things, I started to move away from the shambles of my immediate circumstances and toward a better future.

I've tried to pinpoint the catalyst for my own change, but I honestly can't tell you what started the process. I spoke to friends and family, I briefly worked with a counsellor, and I read countless books. Somewhere in there, the penny dropped. It took me several months to emerge from the depths of my own despair, but emerge I did, and I came out with something I've never lost – a fascination with psychology and the mind that three years at university had failed to instil.

Since then, I've read countless books and academic papers, attended forums and seminars, and spoken to some of the brightest minds. I've basically been a sponge, and it's taught me so many valuable lessons. Yes, it's true, I'm a bit of a geek, but look at this way –I've read all the books, so you don't have to. You just need to read this one– great, eh?

A better mindset for a better future

In the 27 years since graduating from Leeds, my life has taken the usual twists and turns. I've won some, I've lost some, but I've ended up with a life that I love, doing things which make me happy. I have a wonderful wife and three amazing sons. I run a moderately successful business, and I've been able to tackle some crazy challenges – from cycling the length of the UK, to climbing Kilimanjaro twice. (I've even turned my hand to Ironman triathlons, despite reaching my 40th birthday unable to swim).

And all those achievements started with my initial realisations in 1996, and the power of some subtle shifts in my thinking. Just as I turned my own feelings around, so it's possible for you to change how you see the world today.

It takes work, but it can be done, and it *is* worth sticking with.

Of course, in some cases there are more serious issues afoot, and please never hesitate to seek professional advice and guidance if you think you need it. Nothing here will ever be a substitute for getting appropriate medical assistance.

Getting the most from this book

My goal in writing this book is quite simple. In fact, it's been the basis of my business for nearly 20 years: to help ordinary people achieve extraordinary things. I genuinely believe the power to change, and achieve more, lies in every one of us and this book will help you do just that.

In the pages that follow, I'm going to talk you through some of the most important findings from psychologists over the last 50 years. We'll explore the reasons why some people seem to succeed effortlessly whilst others struggle constantly. It's worth saying that, despite how it may seem, it's rarely a matter of luck. It's much more likely to be about mindset meeting action.

We'll look at the evolutionary value of being miserable and consider why we need to break free of our ancestors if we're to achieve our full potential - particularly at times when it seems the world's conspiring against us. At times I'll compare you to a rabbit, a dog, and an elephant – but it'll never be personal.

(Side note: While we're on the subject of animals; a bit of a health warning. Scientific research is vital to better understanding our minds. Unfortunately, much of the research from which we've learned the most, has some slightly whiffy ethical notes. Many experiments have involved animals, and not always in the most pleasant ways. I've included details on this research because it's been important to the subjects I'm discussing, but please don't think that means I agree with the methods. Some experiments were just downright cruel).

This isn't the longest book you'll ever pick up - I've found, over many years of training and tutoring people, long books can be off-putting. Instead, I've tried to distil the important messages into a short, but readable, guide to help you, my lovely reader, bring about lasting change. (If you're really struggling for time, jump to the 'too long, didn't read' summary at the end of each chapter and then work through the chapter exercises).

Let me give you a feel for what's to come. Chapter one looks at why people sometimes feel helpless – and why understanding the ropes that bind you can start the process of setting you free. In chapter two we'll look at hope and expectation and we'll see how the expectations we have for other people (and they have for us) can shape our lives. Chapter three builds on this by considering the importance of the stories we tell ourselves. The world around you is shaped by the way you see it – and the way you see it is shaped by the stories you've told your brain! Chapter four considers the importance of negativity for our ancestors and how you can break free of that evolutionary wiring. Chapter five looks at mindset and considers how your mindset can control not only your results, but maybe even your life expectancy. Our penultimate chapter looks at the hugely important areas of gratitude and mindfulness – areas science is rapidly coming to see as central to our wellbeing. Finally, we'll pull it all together in chapter seven with some additional help to make the change.

The focus is on helping you better understand the way your mind works and giving you new techniques to unlock your own potential, with exercises to help you find the extraordinary person inside. For some of these, you'll need paper and a pen or, if you have a notebook, even better, as you'll be able to flick back to earlier exercises.

So, get ready. Open your mind and prepare to look at your life in a different way. I'm inviting you to take a trip to set you on the path to a happier and more fulfilled life.

Jon Dunckley

July 2023

CHAPTER 1:
BEATEN DOWN

"The loneliest moment in someone's life is when they are watching their whole world fall apart, and all they can do is stare blankly" – F Scott Fitzgerald, The Great Gatsby.

"Most likely lose it again, anyway..." Eeyore – Winnie the Pooh

Elephants in the jungle

IN 2015, MY wife and I took two elephants for a walk. We picked up their thin rope leads and went off through the Thai jungle. These two enormous beasts followed us like puppies, out for their daily stroll around the village. In fact, having walked our two dogs around our local village, the elephants were considerably more obedient. Where we went, they followed.

Now, in the interests of full disclosure, we did have permission – we're not international elephant thieves. We were at a Thai sanctuary, dedicated to the preservation of these wonderful creatures. They charge visitors a hefty fee for the pleasure of taking time with the animals and allow you to walk them, interact with them, and even bathe them, but you can't ride them (quite right too).

About an hour into our jungle trek, we stopped for lunch and let the elephants loose. They happily played in the clearing under our little picnic area, pulling down branches and hitting each other with them, as you do. That was until one of them heard a noise and got spooked. He sounded a warning to his friend, and they ran off to hide… behind a single tree, no more than 18 inches wide. It was quite a sight to see these five-tonne animals using the equivalent of a thin stick for protection, and possibly not the most successful defence strategy, but I digress…

More than the failed effort at hide-and-seek, the most striking thing for me was the way the elephants followed wherever I went, provided I held their thin rope lead. I wondered how the handlers managed to train them so well given their size and talked to our guide about it. He explained that when they're babies, they're attached to their rope. Initially the elephants try to break free but, as they get older, they stop tugging and come to accept they can't. From a young age, little Dumbo and friends just accept the rope as part of their world and they know they need to go where the rope leads. Put simply, they just stop trying.

Image: My friendly elephant – you can see the rope lead behind his ear.

Of course, it's ridiculous to see such an enormous animal held back by a thin rope. It could snap one three times as thick without breaking a sweat. The fact they don't snap the rope tells us a lot about the way the elephant's mind has been programmed, and it also acts as a very powerful metaphor for our own lives.

Just as the elephant is more than capable of breaking free, but doesn't realise it, so you are capable of breaking free from the things holding you back.

See what I did there? The elephant's rope represents your limiting beliefs (this stuff doesn't just throw itself together, you know); and you just need to realise you're being held back. Both the elephant and each of us is confined by the stories of our past and by the beliefs we've built up from our experiences. Like the elephant, there comes a point where you will stop pulling at the rope and accept your lot. But you can break free if you want to.

I should say, in the case of the elephant, the rope does have some value. The sanctuary we visited takes incredible care of its animals, and the rope allows them to handle them more easily. But for humans, this can be one of the most destructive forces. It's called **'learned helplessness'** and it holds back millions of people, preventing them from achieving their full potential.

In the rest of this chapter, I'll talk about how the concept of learned helplessness was first discovered and provide you with some proven strategies for overcoming any learned helplessness 'ropes' that might be holding you back. Once you know the ropes, you can then consider which ones you want to break. You may decide you're happy to be held in place by some of them, but you'd like to shake others off. The goal is to give you the choice, and to make you the controller of your own destiny.

Dogs and shocks

We're going to get a bit 'sciency' here, but it's useful background to understanding how the brain works, so stay with me. Things get lighter as we go through later chapters, so your reward for hanging in there will come!

The concept of learned helplessness was devised by a psychologist called Martin Seligman. He went on to establish the entire field of positive psychology, so you'll hear more about him later, but for now we're looking at his earlier career.

In the 1960s, Seligman was a researcher at the University of Pennsylvania looking at the field of depression. He wanted to find out what caused people to give up and stop trying to change their fate. In the lab where he worked, there were ongoing experiments which involved administering shocks to dogs. Seligman noticed some of the dogs seemed to give up and accept their fate was to be shocked. He wanted to understand why and identify whether there were any links to things he was seeing in depressed people.

In one experiment, run by Seligman and his colleague J.B Overmier[1], three sets of dogs were subjected to different treatment:

- Group one dogs were placed in harnesses and released shortly after

- Groups two and three were connected to each other and given shocks.

  (When I say shocks, I'm not talking a cartoon dog revealing its skeleton as it jumps in the air with hair on end. These were relatively mild sensations, but they were still uncomfortable for the dogs to experience).

The group two dogs had a lever they could tap to end the shocks. The group three dogs also had a lever, but theirs did nothing. Their shocks would only stop when their paired group two dog hit the lever. To this third group, the shocks appeared to come and go at random.

In the next phase of the experiment, all three groups of dogs were placed into a chamber with a dividing wall down the middle. When stood on one side of this divide, they would be shocked but, by making the easy jump to the other side, they could avoid the shock entirely.

Dogs in groups one and two quickly cottoned on to what was required. They worked out the shock wasn't very pleasant and jumped over the divide to get away from it. The dogs from group three – the ones which believed their shocks had been entirely random – simply gave up. They lay down on the floor of the chamber and accepted their lot. They had learned to be helpless. "No point jumping anywhere, the bloke in the white coat's going to shock me whatever I do. May as well just lie down". To these dogs the shocks would come, and they would go, and there was nothing they could do about it, so they didn't even try.

Despite encouraging the group three dogs to jump the barrier with offers of both threat and reward, the researchers couldn't persuade them to move. So deep was their conviction there was no point trying, they lost the willingness to attempt it, even when given a tasty incentive to do so.

In fact, the only thing which proved successful in getting those dogs to jump the barrier, was the researchers picking them up and moving them. Only when they'd lifted them across the barrier a couple of times, could the dogs see there was freedom on the other side and a way to escape their own issues. They needed a helping hand. (Keep that in mind as you work through this book - help is great and if you've got access to it, take it).

It's easy to see why this has become such an important piece of work for the study of personal growth and development. When you feel your circumstances are out of your control and you can't influence what's going on around you, it's easy for anyone to develop learned helplessness.

That said, given you're not a dog, you might be wondering how all this relates to you. Great question, glad you asked. Seligman's work was applied to humans by follow up studies conducted by Donald Hiroto at Oregon State University[2]. Humans don't much like being shocked, so he had to find a more palatable method of looking at how learned helplessness impacts people, and whether it applies equally to everyone.

His solution? He sat participants in a room and played uncomfortably loud music at them. All they had to do was find a way of stopping the music using the panel of buttons in front of them. Of course, for one group of participants, no matter what buttons they pressed, nothing was going to stop the music. A second group of participants were able to stop the noise with the right combination of buttons, while a third group had no noise at all.

These three groups were then put into a second scenario where they placed their hand into a box with a divide down the middle and were subjected to an irritating whooshing noise. All they had to do to stop the noise was move their hand to the other side of the box – much like the dogs had to jump the divide. What Hiroto found, however, was two-thirds of those who'd been in the group with no control over the noise in the first stage just sat there. They didn't look for a way to stop the noise, they accepted their fate.

This experiment is interesting for two reasons. Firstly, it shows learned helplessness can apply to humans just as it applies to dogs. Secondly, the results showed that although two-thirds of the 'helpless' group did nothing, one third didn't succumb to their helplessness, instead they looked for a solution. This gives us grounds for optimism.

Back to the elephants

We will come back to the reasons why those people were able to escape the apparent helplessness later. For now, I just want to jump back to the elephants. Think about learned helplessness in your own life as being like the elephant's rope. In many cases it's something you can break free from if you want to and if you're shown the way. As you continue to read this book, you'll look closely at your mindset and internal beliefs, and you'll also be able to work out which 'ropes' you want to lose, in order to help you achieve more.

Of course, there will be some causes which can't be solved so easily, in which case I do want to emphasise the importance of seeking professional help. If your circumstances are dire and you really can't see a way forward, seek support either from your doctor or another relevant professional.

The ties binding you

How does learned helplessness manifest itself in our everyday lives? Well, there's a spectrum here, from very serious issues needing clinical assistance, right through to minor problems which can be overcome with personal change. To repeat, I won't be dealing with those serious clinical issues here, but I will help you see the everyday ways our own minds can hold us back.

To demonstrate what I mean, and the kind of issues this book is designed to tackle, look at the case studies below, these (and the other case studies you'll read) are all real people I've worked with. Names have been changed for confidentiality:

Case study 1.1: Mae's sales lull

Mae works in sales. She's done incredibly well over the last couple of years and received significant praise and accolades from her employer. Last year, she won the coveted salesperson of the year award, and her manager was talking about a possible promotion to sales manager next time an opening arose.

Unfortunately, Mae's experiencing a bad run of form. Her last six months' figures are well down from her previous level. Instead of praise, her most recent one-to-one meeting was an entirely negative affair where she felt berated.

When the dip started, she made more phone calls and tried to drive more business with existing clients, but it hasn't seemed to work. Three months ago, she started to question her ability. Had she previously been lucky? Was her past success the true version of her, or is this new version more accurate?

The more thought she's given it, the more she's questioned her own ability. She's now decided she isn't ready for management – after all how can she lead people if she can't do the job herself?

As her confidence has waned, she's made fewer calls, has seen fewer people, and the spiral of negative results has continued. She's now decided the only option is to move jobs and she's been pushing her CV around the industry looking for alternative employment.

Case study 1.2: Jackson's struggle with weight

Jackson has never been what people would describe as thin, but he used to be quite athletic. He carried a few extra pounds but was fit and he felt good. He'd do parkrun (a community-based 5km run) on a Saturday morning and always finished in the middle of the pack. A solid runner but, mostly, he did it for fun.

Unfortunately, when the world shut down for Covid, parkrun was cancelled. Jackson found himself furloughed with nothing much to do. Like many people he ended up binge-watching TV and snacking.

Jackson put on a couple of stone in all and, despite trying several of the most popular diets, nothing seems to have worked. He's reached a stage where he's starting to believe that, at 40, his metabolism has slowed, and the weight is never going to come off.

He doesn't run anymore. He tried to go back to parkrun when things opened again, but he was no longer in the middle of the field. All the people he used to run with seemed so much faster than him. He's lost the love of running and these days gets very little exercise other than an occasional walk around town.

Case study 1.3: Harriet's problems with study

Harriet works as an administrator for a firm of financial advisers. She's a huge asset to the team, well liked and highly respected by her colleagues. At her recent one-to-one meeting, her manager suggested she might like to consider training to become an adviser. She told Harriet she could see in her all the attributes of a great adviser and the firm would be willing to help fund her through her studies.

As much as Harriet would love to be an adviser, she told her manager she didn't think it was a good idea. She said she loved doing what she was doing now, but the truth is she was worried about the exams. She tried to take one of them in the past and failed. Admittedly, she did it alone and without any support but, even so, a failure is a failure. When she looked at the advisers in the firm, they all seemed so much cleverer than her. They appeared to sail through the exams, so if she couldn't even pass the first one, what's the point in trying?

The link to learned helplessness

In each case study, it's the limiting beliefs the person holds which stopped them progressing. Each lacked belief in their ability to achieve their goals. They didn't see they had sufficient control over their lives to be able to bring about the changes they wanted and so they accepted their lot.

Rather than concentrating on all the success she'd had in the past, Mae took the view her past success was the unusual situation, rather than her current sales lull. Jackson looked at his weight-gain as being metabolic and as a result decided he couldn't influence it. He stopped doing the parkruns he enjoyed because he couldn't run alongside his old running partners anymore. He didn't see his slower times as a stimulus to run more, quite the opposite in fact. Equally, Harriet took her initial failure in one exam to reflect her chances in all exams. She wrote off her chances of passing before she'd given herself the opportunity to have a go.

Each of these people had the power to turn things around and to achieve more. They just needed to help to look at things differently.

The danger of helplessness

The three people in the case studies are all failing to achieve their full potential, because they believe they aren't capable of more. Things that have happened in the past have convinced each of them there's no point trying to get to the next stage. They've become convinced the matter's out of their control.

Of course, there's no reason why those three people should be held back. Each of them is more than capable of breaking through the barrier and pushing on to hit their goals, but this doesn't diminish the effect their helplessness has on their everyday lives.

The problem is, once someone starts to experience the effects of learned helplessness, it can become self-perpetuating. The more you believe you're incapable of achieving things, the more evidence you'll find to back up this belief. We'll look more at this principle in chapter two, Hope for More, but for now let's think about the implications of this spiral.

If you believe that no matter what you do, the result's going to be the same, what happens to motivation? Of course, it's going to drop off a cliff. If the outcome is predetermined then, just like Seligman's dogs, there seems no point in trying. This pattern plays out millions of times every day, all around the world.

With a fall in motivation comes a rise in your level of stress. You know you should be able to achieve more and become increasingly frustrated that you aren't. Perhaps it has an impact on your ability to earn money, as you saw in Mae's case study. A couple of bad months' sales stops being a blip and instead becomes a sign she's a bad salesperson.

It could impact your ability to push on toward the promotion you want, like it does for Harriet. The more stressed you become, the more serious the potential impact on your long-term health. As if this weren't enough, you start to believe your own stories. You accept your failure is truth —you can't do more, and your self-esteem falls. Before you know it, your entire quality of life can be impacted.

Remember, this is at the lower end of the spectrum. The further up the spectrum of learned helplessness you go, the more serious the potential implications – from staying with an abusive partner, through to long-term psychological conditions.

So, let's return to those one-in-three human participants who didn't succumb to learned helplessness in the Hiroto study. What was it that made them try to change their circumstances?

Well, after much further research, it appears there are three elements to your mindset when it comes to learned helplessness – and these are three legs of the stool you need to attack:

1. **Permanence** – if you believe things are this way forever, you're more likely to give up. You'll be more likely to use language like, "it never works" rather than, "I'm struggling with this one".

2. **Pervasiveness** – the more widely you perceive a problem is impacting your life, the less control you feel you have, and the more significant it's likely to be for you. Phrases like, "I'm stupid" rather than, "I can't understand this…" are common here.

3. **Personalisation** – finally, if you blame yourself for things that go wrong, you're more likely to struggle. Whilst it isn't always right to blame other people, always taking everything on yourself can be very damaging.

As you'll see later, all three of these can be changed – it comes down to the stories you tell yourself and the way you programme your mind.

Exploring your own ropes

Throughout this book we're going to look at some of the most empowering techniques for taking back control of your life and breaking the ropes you no longer wish to be bound by. The problem is you need to recognise they're there in the first place before you can break free of them.

Many of us are held in place by limiting beliefs we don't even know exist. Fear of failure, negative self-talk, imposter syndrome, self-doubt, they're all potentially ropes you can break. You've learned to be helpless without recognising you've become helpless.

Think about it. Did Mae know she was suffering from learned helplessness and recognise she could break the rope and turn her career around again? Did Jackson realise he was attributing his weight gain to his metabolism when it was really down to his changed behaviour? Did Harriet get she was stopping herself from the opportunity to start passing her exams because she was making assumptions based on a single failure from the past?

Before we go on to look at changing things, it's important you find your own ropes, so let's start with a few simple exercises.

Putting it into practice

Exercise 1.1 – introspection

Take time to sit quietly and think about times in your life when you've felt like you were powerless, or when things felt out of your control. Take yourself back to the situation as vividly as you can. What can you see and hear? Paint a clear mental picture of yourself returning to the same thoughts and feelings. This exercise should feel a little like stepping back into the skin of the person you were then.

Now, write down the thoughts that come to your head. Pay particular attention to those related to your abilities, potential, or (lack of) control over your life. Were there ways in which you felt the situation was going on around you? What beliefs did you have in that moment? How did those beliefs impact on the way you approached the situation?

For now, you're looking for what ropes might be holding you back, but we'll come back to these again later and consider how you can change those negative thoughts.

Exercise 1.2 – belief quadrants

Divide a clean sheet of paper up into four quadrants. In each quadrant write one of the following:

- **Family** –your immediate family, the ones you feel closest to

- **Social relationship**s – your friends and social acquaintances

- **Work** – this could be paid or voluntary work

- **Interests** – hobbies, pastimes, things you do for fun

Work through the quadrants one by one, writing down any limiting beliefs you have about yourself in that area. For example, if you feel you don't give enough time to your spouse, write that under family. If you feel you're out of your depth at work, that would go in the work quadrant.

Once you've done that, it's time for the important bit. Take each limiting belief you've identified and question its validity. Ask yourself: "Is this belief based on evidence, or past experiences, or is it a generalization?"

In other words, if you're saying you're a bad spouse, what is this based on? Are you basing it on a long-term pattern of neglecting the one you love the most, or did you just forget one anniversary? If you feel like a failure at work, is it a fair assessment, or have you just missed a deadline recently?

Set aside around 30 minutes for this exercise – it isn't one to rush. If you get stuck, don't worry – it happens. Just sit with it for a while longer, you'll often be surprised how things just pop into your mind. I do also know this can be tough – I'm asking you here to think about some pretty heavy stuff, and we've not even been for dinner together, but this is a safe environment and it'll help with what comes later.

Take each of the things you've written down and challenge them for a more positive alternative. Ask yourself whether I would take the same impression of you if I saw the evidence, or whether you're being harsh on yourself. Now keep these safe – you'll need them when you come to start writing new stories later.

Exercise 1.3 – your trusted friend

This exercise takes some courage and someone you really trust. You're going to open up and make yourself vulnerable here, so it needs to be someone you know has your best interests at heart. If you don't have anyone you feel comfortable being vulnerable with in this way, skip this one.

Share your experiences and your beliefs about yourself with your trusted person. Ask them to act as a sounding board, challenging you on what might be self-limiting beliefs. Look together and work out which are the helpful and which are the limiting beliefs.

If you don't feel ready to do this exercise just now, don't worry, I know many people I've worked with found it tricky at first. You can always come back to it later but, of all the exercises in this book, this one often yields the most powerful insights, so it is worth considering.

It's important you do this exercise when you have time for it and try to do it in a quiet place where you won't worry about other people overhearing. You're going to be sharing your deepest thoughts, after all.

If you haven't yet done so, I recommend completing exercise two before this chat. Then use the quadrants to ask your trusted friend to help you explore whether your beliefs are fair and useful.

Sometimes this exercise will show there really are areas of your life in which you need to put the hard work. Perhaps you could be a more present parent, perhaps you've taken your eye off the ball at work. That's not a bad thing – it all builds toward helping you to move forward. You'd be surprised, though, how often your friend doesn't recognise the person you're describing as being the person they know, and so help you challenge your limiting beliefs.

As you work through the rest of the book, you'll find more exercises to help challenge any unhelpful self-limiting beliefs and replace them with new, more empowering ones. After all, if you want to go on a journey, it's always a good idea to know where you're starting from.

'Too long; Didn't read' chapter summary

An elephant can be trained to walk on a lead simply by putting it one a rope when it's too small to break free. Before it grows strong enough to snap it, the elephant gives up trying and accepts the lead as its reality.

Human beings are prone to the same action. Events that happen to you shape how you perceive the world around you. When things don't go your way and you feel out of control of the situation, you're much more likely to fall prone to giving up.

Psychologist Martin Seligman called this phenomenon 'learned helplessness', the process by which people decide they lack the control over the issues facing them and simply give up trying.

Learned helplessness exists on a spectrum, from relatively minor issues which hold you back from achieving your maximum potential, through to causing some people serious psychological problems needing expert help.

The first step in addressing the low-level learned helplessness is to recognise you have it. A good exercise in achieving this is to sit down with a blank piece of paper and write down everything you believe about yourself under the headings of family, social life, work, and interests.

When you've written down those current beliefs, re-visit them and ask which ones are helpful. Which would choose to believe if you had a completely clean slate, and which ones are less than helpful?

It's those on the second list which will form the basis of our work from chapter two.

CHAPTER 2:
HOPE FOR MORE

"Remember that hope is a good thing, Red, maybe the best of things, and no good thing ever dies." –Stephen King, Rita Hayworth and the Shawshank Redemption.

"Faith, Hop, and Charity... and the greatest of these is Hop." - Arnold J. Rimmer – Red Dwarf

TWO OF THE most powerful forces impacting human lives are hope and expectation. Even a little ray of hope can shift the mind-set a long way from the depths of despair, toward a more empowered position. and have long-term impacts on our ability to withstand troubles.

In this chapter, we'll look at why hope is such a powerful force, and then go on to consider how the expectations in our lives can be either our super-power or our prison. Hope, after all, is just the expectation of better things to come. We'll look at examples of people who've achieved incredible success, and also identify more modest changes we can each relate to.

We'll see how the expectations we place on ourselves, and those placed on us by others, are hugely important in determining our outcomes. A kind word here or there can totally change your outlook. A belief you can achieve great things can galvanise you into action and bring about powerful change. And both can start to create more positive perspectives.

Drowning rats

It's unfortunate that once again, some of the most powerful research is some of the least palatable from an ethical perspective. In this case, the scientist in question is Curt Richter, a biologist, psychobiologist, and geneticist from the USA.

In one famous experiment[1], he placed 34 wild rats into buckets filled with water. As wild rats are naturally good swimmers, they were expected to survive a long time, but there was a twist. The experiment was designed to remove hope from these animals. They had their whiskers removed and were transferred directly from a dark bag into the water, with no indication of there being any way out. The result of this rather unpleasant twist was the rats swam for very little time before giving up and succumbing to the water. None lasted more than a handful of minutes before drowning. The cause of death was cited as heart failure, but not due to speeding up of the heart in panic. Rather, their hearts effectively slowed down and stopped – they lost the will to fight. Richter then looked to establish what might happen if they were given a small glimmer of hope.

In the next phase of the experiment, a further sample of wild rats were subjected to same immersion in water, but this time without having their whiskers removed and, importantly, they were lifted from the water just before they drowned. They moved these poor little fellas in and out of the water several times, drying them off, giving them a short respite, and then re-introducing them into the water. The rats came to believe there was a chance of rescue.

With restored hope, the rats survived for longer – much longer. Some were able to continue swimming for up to 80 hours, just waiting for someone to reach in and pluck them to safety. That's a staggering increase in swimming time. From a few minutes to several days of continuous swimming, with the only difference being a hope that the ordeal would come to an end.

OK, so that's all very well and good, but it's about rats in water. What does it have to do with human beings? The answer is, rather a lot.

Charles Snyder[2] describes hope as comprising two elements – willpower and way power. In other words, we need to see a way forward, and have the will to take the necessary action to get there.

Research using Snyder's measures[3] found veterans suffering from post-traumatic stress disorder (PTSD) achieved better long-term outcomes if they had higher hope scores midway through their treatment. Seeing the light at the end of the tunnel really did help.

Similarly, Nicholas Kristof [4], describes a randomised trial of economic aid involving 21,000 people across six countries. The trial demonstrated aid packages gave poor families significant boosts which continued after the programme ended. Just a small gift of a "Cow. Or a few goats. Even Bees", would yield lasting long-term impacts. That small gift of aid gave people, who'd been feeling hopeless and stuck in a cycle of poverty, some 'way power'. When combined with their willpower, it showed them a way forward.

Placebo and nocebo

A key element of hope is having some belief better things are coming. Many studies have shown what you expect determines your outcomes – both good and bad – with the power to change, or even take, your life. If you give up you expect bad things to happen to you and, just as it did with Richter's rats, the research shows it's likely to lead to bad outcomes.

To help you understand this more, in the Expectation Effect[5] David Robson introduces the concepts of 'placebo' and 'nocebo' and their role in our lives. Most people are aware of the placebo effect - a treatment which appears to be real but is designed to have no real therapeutic impact. Often, this involves giving the patient a sugar tablet or saline injection but telling them the treatment's a real drug designed to achieve a specific outcome.

Of course, there are once again ethical considerations in providing someone with a fake drug whilst telling them it's real, so this approach is most widely used in clinical trials, where a control group is administered a placebo, while the test group receives the drug being tested.

What's incredible, though, is even where the patient is told the drug is a placebo, many still see demonstrable effects. This so-called 'open-label' placebo should intuitively have no effect – the patient is quite aware it's fake – yet the effect of treatment is still seen[6].

Psychologist Irving Kirsch suggests the effect arises because the placebo creates an expectation in the patient's mind, which then becomes self-fulfilling[7]. You're told the drug will cure your headache and you create a set of beliefs in your mind. These persist for some people even if this information is followed up with a contradictory statement (like, "this is a placebo") and sets about a chain of physiological effects in the body which lead to the expected outcome anyway. In other words, the body responds to the expectation we've given it.

While the concept of the placebo effect is well known, its lesser-known sister is even more significant. The 'nocebo' effect is the reverse of the placebo. It shows that if we believe something has the power to do us harm – even when there's no real reason for us to think that way, the outcome can still be negative.

In test of the nocebo effect, patients are given the same inert substance used in the placebo experiments, but this time they're told there will be side-effects. Very often, the individuals then go on to experience these. This negative impact has been shown in multiple drug trials, where participants have suffered the side effects associated with the clinical drug but were only administered the inert control substance[8].

The range of conditions associated with nocebo are vast. One study found evidence of everything from nausea and stomach pains, to itching, bloating, depression, and even severe hypotension[9]. Meanwhile a study in 2022 found the nocebo effect could account for up to 72% of the adverse effects experienced by patients after the first dose of the Covid vaccine[10]. That is a staggeringly high percentage. Almost three quarters of all the effects being reported for the first dose of the vaccine could potentially be the result of a mere expectation bad things would happen. The more reports we read, the more we approach the vaccine with trepidation and the more we create an expectation which becomes self-fulfilling. (Note to self: stop reading the drivel people put on Facebook, and if they're wearing a tin-foil hat, probably best ignore them).

David Robson highlights even more extreme cases – one in particular where a man diagnosed with an incurable condition and given one year to live, died as expected around a year later, only for an autopsy to reveal there was nothing which should have killed him. The diagnosis was wrong. The poor chap didn't have a life limiting condition at all, but the expectation his life was going to be cut short became self-fulfilling.

We see this effect of expectation played out every day. Henry Ford famously said, 'Whether you think you can, or you think you can't, you're right' and he was spot on. Yoda said, 'Do or do not, there is no try' and he was on the money too!

In chapter three we'll talk about the stories we tell ourselves, and the effect these have, but it's important to know the starting point for it all is expectation.

Changing expectations

On the 6 May 1954, a young British runner called Roger Bannister became the first person in history to run a mile in under four minutes, clocking in at 3.59.4. The significance of this run was huge. Until this point, many experts – including physiologists – had argued it was physically impossible for someone to run a mile in less than four minutes. The commonly held belief was the human body would break under the strain. In other words, the existing record was already considered the peak of performance.

Bannister wasn't willing to accept such a limitation, and, with the help of pacers, he went out and broke the assumed barrier.

What's most significant about this, though, isn't the performance of one man, but the results which followed. In the period between Bannister's record-breaking run and April 2021, some 1664 other people have also broken the four-minute mark, and at the time of writing the current record is some 7% faster at 3.43.13.

Now, of course, you can argue training methods have improved, equipment is better, tracks are designed to create more spring and drive better times, and all of these are valid points. But what if we go right back to the 1950s when everyone was training and racing in the same conditions as Bannister?

Within 13 months of Bannister's race, four other people ran a mile in under four minutes. Within 4 years, the number had risen to 18. The conditions hadn't changed dramatically. What had changed was the belief and expectation of the runners. Before Bannister, people assumed the four-minute mark to be impossible. After Bannister, that expectation had been taken away.

This same effect has played out in my own family. My son is a good runner. From an early age we'd take him to parkrun on a Saturday morning and by 13 he was running in the front of the pack, but then he hit a wall. He couldn't break the 19-minute mark. However hard he tried, however much he trained, 19 minutes and a handful of seconds was the best time he could reach for the 5k distance…until we introduced a change. I suggested he run without his watch. I said he should just run, enjoy the effort, and that he should give it his best shot but not worry about the time. You can probably work out what happened...

Without the watch to check himself against, he was no longer confined by his limiting expectations. He smashed through the mental ceiling he'd placed on himself and within a few months achieved his best time in the 16 minutes bracket. It was his limiting belief which had held him back, not his ability. (Although, I'll admit, sometimes I wish I hadn't bothered – I can't keep up with him now).

Both these examples are based on running, but the effect extends across all aspects of life. Consistently, we find it isn't our ability which shapes our outcomes, rather it's our expectations of the outcomes. I've worked with many people who've struggled with public speaking. When I ask them to talk me through their fears, they invariably talk about everybody laughing at them and judging them, causing them to perform badly. When the time comes to stand on the stage, sure enough, they don't present as well as they can. But is anyone laughing at them? Well, other than in the right places when they make jokes, no. People aren't judging them either. Their performance is simply damaged by their expectation they'll perform badly. They've created their own reality and made their perspective into their prison.

The Pygmalion effect – changing the lives of others

It's clear, then, what you believe, you can achieve. But research suggests the truth goes beyond this – not only what you believe, but what other people believe and expect of you (and what you expect of other people) can also have a huge part to play.

In mythology, Pygmalion was a Cypriot sculptor who fell in love with his statue, Galatea. So strong was his love for the statue that Aphrodite, the goddess of love, gave him his wish and made the statue real. (I'd love to pretend I knew that without looking it up...)

Now, since this isn't a book on Greek mythology, there must be a point lurking in here somewhere and here it is - the 'Pygmalion effect'. This suggests simply having someone who believes in your ability to succeed increases your chances of success. Like Pygmalion's belief in the statue was enough to bring about an altered reality, so the expectations you place on others, or which others place on you, have the power to change reality too.

Robert Rosenthal and colleagues did research into this at Jacobson's elementary school in California, way back in 1968 (resulting in some people referring to the 'Rosenthal effect' rather than 'Pygmalion effect')[11]. Rosenthal and his team put all the children through a standardised IQ test and collated the results. They then presented the school with a list of high achievers; children they described as 'intellectual bloomers.' In other words, these were the children who could be expected to achieve great progress in the coming year.

When they returned twelve months later and once again gave all the students the same test they'd taken at the start of the study, their predictions proved accurate. Those children singled out as potential high achievers did show above-average performance improvements.

But there was a catch here. The children on the high achievers list were selected at random. Some of them had indeed performed well in the test, others had performed badly. They hadn't been the top performers on the test at all, just 20% selected by chance – a cunning trick Dr Rosenthal, well played.

Rosenthal argued the expectation created by the list, in the minds of the teachers, acted as a self-fulfilling prophecy. Although investigation suggested they hadn't spent more time with the potential high performers (in some cases they'd actually spent less time with them), they had raised their expectations for the selected cohort of children. They'd set them more difficult tasks, asked more of them, and given them more opportunity to grow. It was Rosenthal's belief teachers were acting subconsciously to deliver better outcomes for those students who they believed had higher potential. The expectation the teachers held went on to impact the outcomes the children achieved.

Although this study has its critics, it's been widely recognised as one of the most important in the field of expectation and outcomes, and it raises interesting questions: How often do other people's expectations of you have a bearing on your output? How often do the expectations you place on other people have an impact on them?

Many of you reading this will have children, many will employ other people. Are you creating expectations for your children and your employees? How positive are those expectations?

As positive as the Pygmalion effect can be, you do need to be careful of the downside. Just as you can create positive outcomes by believing in people, sometimes you can create negative outcomes by having a negative impression of people. This is sometimes called the 'reverse Pygmalion effect' or the 'Golem effect'.

Equally, what impact do the people around you have on your own wellbeing? If you have a manager who tells you a promotion isn't for you, what does this do to your belief in yourself, and your own outcomes?

This idea of expectations leading to an outcome for other people is shown in the following case studies:

Case study 2.1- Driving Mary

Mary is 55 years old. She'd never driven a car. Throughout her life, she relied on other people for transport, whether it be public transport or help from friends and family.

We recently talked about the reasons why she's never driven, and she told me she didn't really know what stopped her. "There have been many times in my life where I've thought about it, but for some reason I've never got started".

The more we explored it, the clearer the real reason became. She had spoken about it with her ex-husband many years ago, and he'd told her she had such bad co-ordination, she'd 'never be able to drive'. Any time people had asked why she didn't drive, he'd close off the subject with a throwaway line about it not being 'her thing'.

Objectively, there was no reason to assume this was the case. She regularly cycles with groups of friends and holds her place in a large group of cyclists quite comfortably. No-one has ever noticed any co-ordination issues, and she doesn't think of herself as being some-one who lacks co-ordination.

Her ex-husband's belief she couldn't drive, and his expecta-tion she'd fail, translated itself into her reality.

Finally, at 55, she's looking at driving lessons.

Case study 2.2 – Meera's career

Meera is a doctor, a great doctor. Her patients love her, and her colleagues seem to love her even more.

She doesn't remember a time when there was another career ahead of her. "I was always going to be a doctor," she told me, "Mum and Dad had planned it out from before I was born". Their child would be a doctor, this was just a given.

"As I grew up, they would take me to exhibitions and museums, they'd buy me books on the way the body worked. They were never 'in my face' about it, it was normal to us. I was going to be a doctor, end of discussion".

Meera's parents had set high expectations for her. They believed she could be a doctor even before they'd met her. Everything that happened thereafter was driven by their expectations. Meera never questioned whether she had the ability to become a doctor. To her, that would have been like questioning whether she had the ability to breathe.

In both these case studies, the outcome was determined, at least in part, by the belief of other people. In the first, the negative attitudes of Mary's husband contributed to feelings of self-doubt and created a downward spiral. In the second, the positivity of Meera's parents passed on the belief that change was possible.

Think creatively

One final point before we move on to some exercises. In his book The Third Door[12], Alex Banayan talks about the third door which nightclubs have. Everyone knows about the 'normal' door – the one at which most people queue. They also know about the VIP entrance, where the lucky few get invited to enter. But fewer people know about the third. The one down the dingy alley. The rusting metal door down by the bins where, if you bang hard enough, you'll get admitted through the kitchen. OK, maybe it won't work in all nightclubs, but the point is, don't just take what you know on face value. If you look for the third way, you might just find it.

Why does this matter? Well, research has shown a link between thinking creatively and increased levels of hope. The more creative you can be, the more hopeful you can become.

Putting it into practice

In the next chapter, we'll build on the idea of expectation by considering the power of the stories you tell yourself and how you can program your brains to help you achieve more. Before we get to that, though, let's think about how you can draw out some of the expectations currently holding you back.

Exercise 2.1 – Pygmalion in the real world

Let's start by considering the views you hold about yourself and others, and the impact this has. For this exercise, divide a blank sheet of paper in two with a horizontal line across the middle of the page.

In the top section, write, "Things people believe about me". Then put "Things I believe about other people" in the bottom half of the page.

Start with whichever half you prefer. All you need to do is write the belief and who it's about. So, for example, you might write about one of your team, "He's a bit lazy". Alternatively, you might write about the way your biggest client sees you, "She thinks I'm the gift that keeps on giving – she thinks she can call me anytime and I'll jump."

Do this without thinking too deeply. The idea is to just dump your thoughts on the page, to get them out there.

When the page is full, revisit each of statement and ask yourself what impact it's having. Which are useful beliefs that help either you or the other person, and which are potentially damaging beliefs?

The useful ones you can keep, the damaging ones you'll aim to replace as you work through the rest of the book, but just naming them can be a big step toward positive action.

Exercise 2.2 – Is there a version?

If you've watched the brilliantly funny TV series 'Staged' with David Tennant and Michael Sheen, you might have seen a particular episode at the start of the third season called, "Is there a version?"

In the show, their writer persuaded them both to join a project they'd already turned down, by asking them, "But, is there a version of this where we do go ahead?"

Although it played out amusingly on the small screen, when you use it with yourself, it's a tremendously powerful way to look at your expectations and consider whether, and how, you might be able to change them.

If you expect yourself to fail, try asking, "Is there a version of this where I succeed and how do I get there?"

Exercise 2.3 – High-five time

This exercise is based The High 5 Habit by Mel Robbins[13]. It's really simple, but it's OK if you're not convinced to begin with. (I'll be honest, I wasn't 100% certain about this one until I tried it and found it worked!)

Mel argues high performing teams are regularly seen giving each other 'high fives.' If you've ever watched cricketers batting, they seem to stroll down the wicket after every ball to touch gloves. Basketball players high-five after every play and tennis doubles players fist-bump as standard. In each case, there's a powerful connection formed. The simple action of the high five serves to raise your mood and make you feel better. Her suggestion? Give yourself a high five in the mirror every morning.

Even if you aren't sure, give it a try for a week or two and note the impact it has on your mood. Some people describe feeling more positive, more open, and even more 'alive'. It takes no time at all, and the results can be so uplifting, so what do you have to lose?

Exercise 2.4 – The third door

Imagine a table. On it, is a jug of water and an empty glass. I take the jug and fill the glass with water to the half-way point. Then I ask you to tell me what you see. What would you say? Would you describe a glass half empty? Half full? Or would you think about the third door?

What you ought to be looking for, if you want to raise your levels of hope, is that creative third option – a glass which can be topped up at will because there's still a jugful of water on the table.

When you next find yourself confronted with a problem, take some time to consider whether there might be an entirely different way of looking at it. One that could give you a 'third door' option.

If you want to really amplify the effect here, look for your creative solutions to your problems when you're feeling tired. Research quoted by Daniel Pink[14] shows that when you're tired, your inhibitions start to fall, and you open your minds to more creative outcomes.

Exercise 2.5 – help others

One of the most widely proven ways to raise your own hope and expectations, is to help others. The simple act of helping other people can make you feel better about yourself. You don't need to spend a lot of time or invest a lot of money to do it. Just doing something for people who have less than you can make you feel better.

Consider volunteering for a couple of hours a week or look at making micro-loans of up to $25 to small businesses in the developing world through an organisation like Kiva (www.kiva.org). Then reflect on how the act made you feel.

'Too long; didn't read' chapter summary

Hope is a powerful driver. Experiments have shown when it's removed, outcomes are significantly worse. Just introducing some hope into your life can open you up to the possibility of better outcomes, which can result in positive change.

Hope is about belief and expectation. What you expect to happen can determine your eventual outcomes. The placebo effect has been shown to deliver medical benefits from inert substances where the patient believes the drug will be effective. Bizarrely, even if the patient's told the drug is a placebo, it can still have these positive outcomes, because the physiological chain of events has been set off.

The opposite of the placebo effect is the nocebo effect. This shows that if you believe bad things will happen to you, very often this becomes a self-fulfilling prophecy (just like the placebo effect does for positive outcomes).

What you believe of others and what others believe of you has long-term implications for our success. The so-called Pygmalion effect shows when people have high expectations for you, you're more likely to achieve positive outcomes. Equally, when you believe in other people, they're more likely to succeed.

By cultivating hope and challenging your expectations, you can not only turn things around for yourself, but also for other people. But you do need to critically assess what expectations other people are placing on you and how this impacts your life.

You can improve your outcomes by reframing how you see the world around you and looking for alternative versions. This can be enhanced by thinking about the out of the ordinary options you might have missed (the third door).

Literally high fiving yourself has been shown to enhance mood, while taking time to consider the expectations you're putting on yourself and others, (and the impacts they're putting on you), can show you areas where change can yield benefits.

CHAPTER 3:
THE STORIES WE TELL...

"There's always room for a story that can transport people to another place." – *J.K. Rowling*

"My name? Yes, it's J. R. Hartley" – *Yellow Pages*

THE HUMAN BRAIN is an incredible thing. With up to 100 billion neurons, each able to connect to as many as 100,000 other neurons, we're talking about a machine that can make 100 trillion connections. And these connections aren't static, they constantly adapt, physically reshaping our internal wiring on a moment-to-moment basis.

In fact, the grey matter we carry around with us is still the most complex thing in the known universe. Imagine that. For all the wonderous things we've discovered both on Earth and outside the planet, there's still nothing yet as complicated or awe-inspiring as the contents of your head. From the minute you were born until the moment you draw your last breath your brain works 24-hours a day. It interprets the world around you, controls how you interact with it, and regulates the body to keep you safe. And it does all this on around a tenth of the power used by the computer on which I'm typing these words. How's that for energy efficiency? Clever, and eco-friendly, what's not to love?

Despite this complexity, it's surprising how many short-cuts the brain takes in its quest to look out for you. These short-cuts, or 'heuristics', often result in the brain making big decisions based on an incredibly small amount of information. Mostly, those decisions work out fine, but sometimes you'll get it wrong. When this happens, the short-cut becomes a 'cognitive bias', which can cause loss of hope and learned helplessness.

A cognitive bias is a systematic error in the way you think, which can cause problems with the way you perceive reality. Your brain is constantly making big decisions, and often without any involvement from your conscious mind. Whilst this might be effi-cient when things go right, your cognitive biases can result in some bad outcomes and significant unhappiness.

In this chapter, we'll look at the role of stories and how they can determine your outcomes We'll think about the stories you tell your brain, and the shortcuts it creates, the evolutionary value of stories and how marketing has been making use of them since the beginning. We'll also consider the dangers of 'catastrophising' and the reasons you might be so prone to doing so and look at strate-gies to give yourself more empowering stories.

Having spent time getting to grips with the concepts of learned helplessness and the impact of hopelessness, consider this chapter the real start of your fight back against things which have been holding you back.

It's time to create the stories you want to have.

The story-telling ape

We live in a complex world. The average person is exposed to around 75 gigabytes (GB) of 'stuff' each day. Whether from TV, radio, printed press, or books, you're taking on more information than ever before.

To put this in context, just 500 years ago, 75GB is the amount of data a reasonably well-educated person might have expected to consume during their entire life – that's a lifetime of data, every single day[1].

If you think about it, it makes sense. Today there are so many ways to consume data and most people are constantly connected to some form of data provision. Be honest, when you wake up in the morning, do you reach for your phone? I know I do. Do you go to bed still watching or reading something on your phone? Me too.

With the rise of social media, some estimates suggest the amount of data we're consuming is even higher than 75GB, and it's only going to rise further. With apps entirely designed to reward us for constant scrolling, it doesn't take long to clock up the miles (for your finger at least). One study compared social media scrolling to key distances like the height of Everest. It suggested in 2021, the average person's scrolling thumb travelled 0.3888km per day – enough to summit Everest in just over three weeks[2].

To put it another way, your thumb travels more than the height of the Eiffel tower every day. Given this is talking about the average person, it seems safe to assume the younger generation are travelling even further, but whichever way you look at it, it's a lot of scrolling.

As you can see, there's so much 'stuff' surrounding us, the brain needs to limit the amount of information it actively processes. Even 100 trillion neural connections aren't enough to pay active attention to everything that's going on. At any given point in time, we're surrounded by as many as 11-million items of information, yet the human brain can only pay active attention to around 50. This means an awful lot of things need to either be ignored or handled automatically – hence the shortcuts.

These short-cuts (heuristics) are essentially the filters you give your brain, to help interpret the world around you. In the Chimp Paradox[3], Professor Steve Peters talks about the 'programmes' you give the computer of your brain. These programmes then run in the background, making automated decisions for you, without your conscious involvement. Most of the time they'll work just fine (and we'll come back to this concept in more detail in chapter four). If you see a car driving toward you, for example, you know it's a good idea to get out of the way. You don't need to think about that one. Unfortunately, when you combine your heuristics with your cognitive biases though, they can often lead to some unexpected results.

Let's give you an example or two to help this one sink in.

Have a look at the three questions below and make a note of your answers. Don't think too long about each one, just go with what comes to mind:

1. **The bat and ball** – If a bat and ball cost £55, and the bat costs £50 more than the ball, how much does the ball cost?

2. **The Ark** - How many of each type of animal did Moses take onto the ark?

3. **Lilies** - A pond starts off with one lily pad, and every day the number of lily pads doubles. If the entire pond is full in 30 days, how many days did it take for half the pond to be covered?

Most people, when asked these questions will respond with the same answers. The ball must cost £5, there were two of each animal, and if it takes 30 days to cover the pond, it must take 15 to cover half of it. Those are the answers which come from the instinctive, automatic processing part of the brain. Of course, they're also all completely wrong.

If the bat and ball together cost £55 and the bat is £50 more than the ball, the ball can't cost £5. That would make the bat only £45 more expensive. The correct answer is £2.50 for the ball, leaving £52.50 for the bat, which is exactly £50 more.

Equally, although there were two of each type of animal taken on to the Ark (so the story goes) it was Noah who took them there rather than Moses. And if the number of lily pads doubles each day, it was the day before it was full when half the pond would have been covered – day 29, not day 15.

In each of these three cases, consistently you find respondents who don't ponder too long on the question will answer wrongly for one or more questions, as the brain takes shortcuts to get to what is the easiest, if not the correct, response. You can see these short-cuts at work in the real-life examples below:

Case study 3.1 – *The teens in the high street*

I was walking down the high street one night with my wife. It was dark, raining, and the light in town wasn't great.

Walking towards us were three young men with their hoods up. They appeared, at first glance, to be around 15 or 16 years old, and they were talking loudly. My instinctive reaction was to tense up and see them as a threat. I began recalling various martial arts techniques I'd learned years ago, as I prepared to defend us both.

As they got nearer, they started to walk towards us, becoming increasingly vocal. They were pointing and talking excitedly. My heart rate increased – this was going to kick off.

But then they reached us. One of them shrieked with delight and yelled, 'Miss Biggs. I haven't seen you for years!'

My wife, you see, is a former teacher. These children had been in her class and, quite apart from being no threat to us, they were massive fans of hers. They'd have crawled over glass if she'd asked them, and if she'd been in trouble, they'd have been rushing in to defend her, not attack her.

Did I feel stupid when I told my wife what I'd been thinking? Did she give me stick about it? What do you think!

Case study 3.2 – Fear of having children

Jack was determined not to have children. When I raised the subject with him, his face seemed to change, as if he was hardening his resolve. He set his jaw, furrowed his brow, and said, "That isn't going to happen."

It isn't that Jack doesn't like children – he does. He's a great uncle and he's a great older brother. He just didn't think he wanted to have any kids of his own.

Jack's number one driver for not having children was a deep-rooted belief he'd be a terrible father. He'd made up his mind he didn't have what it takes to be a good dad, and he had no intention of "putting a child through that". This statement grabbed me and when we explored it further, he told me his own dad had been a terrible father. He'd seldom been there, and when he was, he was either shouting at Jack and his siblings, or at their mum. Jack didn't want to put his own kids through the same misery.

Jack is a gentle, present, man. He cares deeply about the people around him and the last thing in the world I could imagine was him being the kind of father he'd had. Yet his internal story made a short-cut assumption he would have to follow his dad's footsteps if he became a dad himself, so he believed he was better off not bringing children into the world.

In both these cases, short-cuts led to incorrect assumptions because the brain made potentially big decisions using the lens of the stories it's been told. You'll see this in the case studies throughout this book– poor internal stories leading to bad outcomes. Remember Mae, in chapter one, having a bad time in her sales job? She was telling herself the wrong stories and her brain was latching on to them. Likewise, Harriet, who didn't want to study, was jumping to the conclusion she couldn't pass exams, simply because she'd failed once and created a story based on that.

There are good reasons why your brain develops heuristics, like the assumption I made with the teenagers. There's a safety in taking the conservative option (and we'll look at this in the next chapter), but you can see the impact of the filters you create in something called the 'Baader Meinhof phenomenon'.

You may know Baader Meinhof was a West German far-left terrorist group from the 1970s, so you'd be forgiven for wondering what this could have to do with the stories you tell your brains.

Well...the Baader Meinhof phenomenon was named by Terry Mullen, in 1994[4]. He described a situation where he mentioned the organisation once, sometime after they moved out of the public eye, and subsequently saw their name popping up much more widely. This is similar to everyday experiences we all have, like buying a new car only to suddenly see that model of car everywhere, or the way social media seems to send you adverts for the very things you were discussing with your friends in the pub.

In 2005, Stanford Linguistics professor, Arnold Zwicky took the Baader Meinhof phenomenon and instead coined the term 'frequency illusion'[5] which more effectively sums up the situation.

In the above examples, the number of occurrences doesn't change. There were no more mentions of Baader Meinhof after Mullen mentioned them than there had been before. New cars hadn't suddenly flooded the road and, despite what the conspiracy theorists might tell you, Big Brother isn't listening to you in the pub. All that's happened is your filters have changed. By first talking about Baader Meinhof, Terry Mullen had opened up the filters in his brain to allow mentions of them through into his consciousness. In other words, he'd told the brain this was no longer to be considered spam. He'd created a new heuristic.

Think for a second about the implications of this. How much of the world around you is being automatically filtered out without your conscious mind ever getting involved. How many opportunities that would help you achieve your goals are going begging because you walk right past them?

The question, then, is how do you get past these filters and encourage more of the things you want into your life, while eliminating the things you don't want? Wouldn't it be great if the things that make you unhappy could automatically be filtered out, while the things that have the potential to make you smile like a Cheshire Cat could be sought out with radar-like accuracy and ushered straight through the lens of your consciousness? The good news is it's entirely possible to do this. There's a saying that "neurons that fire together, wire together". In other words, the more we focus on something, the more our brain hardwires it as a filter. We just need to create some new wiring – some new stories.

The brain loves a story

Humans are hard-wired to respond to stories. Society might have evolved a long way, but as we'll see in chapter four, our bodies haven't evolved at the same pace. Our near ancestors didn't have access to the internet, TV, radio (I almost envy them sometimes, no Facetube, no 927 channels of terrible TV, and no endless repeats of Natalie Imbruglia's 'Torn' on Heart radio – what is their obsession with that song?)

The first book, as far as we're aware, was printed less than 3,000 years ago which, in the 200,000 or so years of *homo sapiens'* time on Earth, is a drop in the ocean. For the rest of our existence, we've been reliant on using stories to pass information from one generation to the next.

Around campfires, our ancestors would pass down the collected wisdom of their generation to the ones who followed. Over time, our brains developed an affinity for story as a means of communication. Marketers will tell you that when you hear a story, the neural activity in your brain increases fivefold[6]. If you hear the words 'fly fishing', many people will still think of the Yellow Pages advert with J. R. Hartley, for example. What they don't realise is how old the advert is - it was made in 1983! Equally, for some, the football team Accrington Stanley will forever be associated with Ian Rush and milk, owing to a 1989 advert (Accrington Stanley, who are they? Exactly!). The enduring power of these adverts is down to one common factor – story.

Some of the world's best memory champions utilise stories as a means of helping them remember vast amounts of information – linking the facts they need to remember to items, or destinations in a journey. Seemingly impossible quantities of data can be recalled by linking things in this way.

So, the brain loves – and even needs – story. But here's the important bit - it isn't all that discerning about which stories it takes in. To the brain, one is as good as another, it simply believes whatever you tell it the most. In fact, when it comes to retaining things in your memory, the brain will hold imagined events alongside real events. In other words, if you paint a picture and imagine something happening, your brain will store it as fact. This becomes particularly clear when you speak to someone suffering from dementia.

My own mum has dementia, and she finds it almost impossible to distinguish between the things which have actually happened and those she's imagined. On a recent stay in hospital, she became convinced she'd signed up for a half marathon and needed to get discharged quickly so she could train. If she'd entered, she was doing it – that's the kind of woman my mum is. The fact she's 69 and has two severely arthritic knees didn't cross her mind. Instead, her reality was shaped by her story.

This construction of apparently real events applies whether we're talking about positive or negative situations. If you vividly imagine yourself achieving a goal, your brain stores it as real. As far as the brain's concerned, you really did just win Love Island. Congratulations! Equally, though, if you imagine every possible doomsday scenario and spend your time catastrophising – worrying through the worst-case scenario – your brain will retain that as fact too. You know all those horrible things you imagined were happening? - The brain now thinks they were real.

To demonstrate how this works, one set of researchers[7] showed students a picture of themselves on a hot air balloon during their childhood. They were asked about the day in guided interview. Around 50% of the students were able to describe the event, in some cases down to the people they shared the experience with. The catch? The photos were doctored, and none of the students had ever been on a hot air balloon. The nature of the discussion caused them to combine the apparent photographic evidence, with their imagination, to create false memories. The brain believed what it was told and to those students, the experience of the hot air balloon became a perceived reality. I wonder how they felt when they were told they'd not actually been on a balloon. I'd be gutted. "I've only just remembered an amazing experience and now I've lost it". Doh!

Real or not real?

When you think about the impact of these 'lenses', it's easy to understand why the word 'fear' is said to stand for 'False Expectations Appearing Real'. If you create a terrible imagined situation, you create a perception of reality for your brain to live out. When someone doesn't return your call, you could take a couple of different routes. You could assume they were busy and simply forgot. Or you tell yourself they hate you and didn't return your call because they really want bad things to happen to you.

Taking the opposite angle, of course, using positive visualisation can be an incredibly powerful tool for success. Top class athletes often talk about playing the entire race, or match, through in their mind before it happens. They vividly imagine themselves cantering to victory or overcoming opponents. In their brains, they've already won.

You can see the power of this by doing the following, brief, exercise:

Exercise 3.1 – *The best time of your life*

In chapter one, I asked you to imagine a time in your life when you felt helpless, and life was running away from you. This time, you're going to turn it on its head. This time, I'd like you to go back to a day when you felt completely in control. When everything was going just as you wanted it to. It could be any day – it's your life and your memory – so what's it going to be? Now go back and recall the day in as much detail as you can manage. Feel all the same feelings you felt then. Hear the same sounds, smell the same smells – in other words, immerse yourself in the moment.

Then stay there for a minute or two. Once you've done that, come back to me and carry on reading…

Did you do the exercise? Really? OK, then, let's think about what happened.

What feelings did it produce? What reactions? Did your heartbeat speed up? Did it make your tummy flutter? How light and positive did you feel? How uplifted? Above all else, how different did it feel when compared to the helplessness exercise in chapter one?

If you've been doing the exercises throughout, this is a great time to go back to your notes from exercise 1.1. In that exercise, you were thinking about a time when you'd felt powerless. Both in that exercise and this one, you're experiencing the power of story in your mind. The story from chapter one was you at a low point. It almost certainly brought you down and made you feel helpless. The story you thought about just now should be more empowering. It should make you feel good. It should make you feel in control.

Spend a few minutes just mulling over how different each one made you feel. What different emotions did you experience for each?

Ok, you know where this is going, right?

You have the power to create better realities for yourself by telling yourself better stories. You can change the way you see the stories you already have. You can alter your perspective on events to create more empowering narratives which make you feel better.

The power of perspective

Many of you will have heard of Viktor Frankl. He was an Austrian psychiatrist, who also happened to be Jewish. In 1942, just nine months after he was married, he was sent to a concentration camp along with his family. His father died there, while Viktor and his remaining family were sent to Auschwitz in 1944. His mother and brother were killed in the gas chambers, and his wife died of typhus in Bergen-Belsen. Frankl lived through the most unimaginable horrors, watching his fellow inmates suffer the most humiliating and dehumanising deaths. Yet throughout the experience, Frankl never lost his positivity. He set himself the objective of helping people. It became his mission, and he took each day as a new challenge to help more.

In his incredible book, Man's Search for Meaning[9], Frankl says:

Everything can be taken from a man but one thing: the last of the human freedoms—to choose one's attitude in any given set of circumstances, to choose one's own way.

In other words, the ability to tell yourself different stories,

You can choose how you view the circumstances around you and with it have the potential to create a different life.

There's absolutely no doubt life in a concentration camp is truly horrific. To live through such a dehumanising experience, and yet still choose to find meaning in hardship, shows enormous strength of character and also points toward an important aspect of this conversation – circumstances can be objectively bad, but we can still create a more positive subjective interpretation of them.

Mo Gawdat, former head of Google-X and now happiness campaigner extraordinaire, points to three vital questions you should ask yourself, when confronted with difficulty[9]:

1. Is this objectively real – am I seeing things as they are?

2. Can I change it?

3. Can I live with it and still make the world a better place despite it?

This, in some ways, echoes the 'serenity prayer' used in Alcoholics Anonymous:

Grant me the serenity to accept the things I cannot change,

courage to change the things I can,

And the wisdom to know the difference.

This idea of acceptance and change are vitally important, but before we get to them, we'd best tackle the first of Mo's points – is this objectively real?

Given what you now know about the decisions the brain makes, on limited information, your first port of call when something goes wrong should be to ask yourself whether you've made a mistake. Is what you think is happening, really happening? Your brain is likely to tell you one of two different types of stories:

1. **Positive stories** – the optimistic viewpoint

2. **Negative stories** – the pessimistic viewpoint

We'll look at optimism and pessimism in more detail in chapter five, but for now, the point to recognise is many of the stories you tell yourself naturally stray toward the negative. Have a read of the following case studies and see if they resonate:

Case study 3.3 – the introduction

Peter met someone at a conference and enjoyed an engaging chat. A week later, he received an email from the conference host, formally introducing him to the person he'd been speaking to. The conference host thought the two of them would have a lot in common and should talk more. He replied to all and said how much he'd enjoyed talking, and how much he'd like to carry on the conversation. Two weeks later, he's heard nothing.

Case study 3.4 – redundancies

Carol has worked for her company for nearly five years. Recently, she's had a new manager take over the department and the two of them don't seem to have clicked. This week the company announced there are likely to be redundancies. At her 1-2-1 meeting, her manager asked Carol if she'd be putting her name forward for voluntary redundancy.

Case study 3.5 – the pain in the leg

Sam has been struggling with a pain in his right leg. He's always been active and has run marathons for the last few years, but this pain is stopping him running. He's seen his physio, but she seems stumped. She's suggested he might need an MRI on his back. It could be nothing, but there's a small chance he has problem with his spine which could need surgery. If he does, it will mean the end of his running career, at least for any distance over 5km.

As you read through each of these, what feelings did they produce in you? Did you feel for Peter being 'ghosted'? Were you in 'team Carol' against her boss who seems determined to get rid of her? How about Sam? Did you commiserate with him, losing the running he loves?

Or did you look at it from the other side? Did your mind instantly jump to the conclusion that Peter's contact is probably on holiday, struggling under a huge workload, or simply missed his email? Perhaps it got swept up into a spam filter. Did you look at Carol and assume the manager – and every other manager in the company - was simply asking everyone in the team whether they wanted voluntary redundancy, so they could understand whether they might be able to avoid compulsory job losses? What about Sam – did you concentrate on the small chance he might need a back operation, or the larger chance he won't, and assume he'll be fine?

These case studies provide good examples of 'growth' and 'fixed' mindsets – the subject of chapter five – but the first group of reactions also demonstrate 'catastrophising' – assuming the worst and creating an internal story which blows it out of proportion. It's something we're all prone to do from time to time, but which can have very strong negative consequences.

When you catastrophise, the brain looks at the limited information and applies a 'disaster filter' to assume the worst. Then it plays out, in vivid detail, the potential implications of the worst-case scenario and starts forming battle plans. The more you concentrate on it, the more the neurons fire and start to wire, and as you now know, your brain then creates a perceived reality. You turn the catastrophe into your truth.

What Mo Gawdat is suggesting is that, when faced with these scenarios, we pause. When you start to think you've been ghosted, your boss is trying to get rid of you, or you're about to be ruled out of running for life, take a moment. Look at the facts, not the feelings and ask yourself – 'Is this real'? Do I have enough evidence to jump to the conclusion I'm about to jump to or, is there a version of this scenario where everything's fine? What's the evidence for each case being the truth?

By challenging yourself in this way, you can undertake a process of what psychologists, call 'reframing'. This builds on an extensive body of work by the leading psychologist Aaron Beck, who created the field of cognitive therapy back in the 1960s. He worked with depressed patients to help them look at their troubles in a different way with the outcome that they were able to change their internal stories and create new lenses. In each of the scenarios above, the 'optimistic' view of events was an example of reframing – an alternative possibility offering a more pleasant outcome.

Reframing stress

Most of us have been prone to stress at one point or another in our lives, and we're confronted by almost endless stories of its dangers. But is there another way to frame this? Well, psychologists argue there is.

Let's get a bit 'white-coat and clipboard' for a moment and consider what happens with stress. When you experience it, your body begins a complex series of physiological responses known as the 'stress reaction' or 'stress response'. The key biological players in this process are the hypothalamus and the pituitary gland (both in the brain), and the adrenal glands (which sit just above the kidneys).

The stress reaction begins when the hypothalamus, releases a hormone (CRH) which stimulates the pituitary gland. This, then, releases another hormone (ACTH). Still with me? So that's two hormones now raging around the bloodstream.

From there, ACTH travels to the adrenal glands, which respond by releasing stress hormones, primarily in the form of cortisol. Cortisol has various effects on the body. It increases blood sugar levels, suppresses the immune system, and enhances the availability of glucose to provide energy for the body to respond to whatever horrible event is about to befall it.

All this happens quickly and is designed to help you prepare for immediate action in threatening situations. The problem, is, as you know, most of the things which cause you stress aren't immediate, and you don't always want to fight or run away from them. The effect of this? Your body continuously releases these powerful hormones, creating a pattern of chronic stress which can have significant negative impacts on both your physical and mental health - not cool.

So how can stress still be good? Well, this is where things get interesting. Positive psychologist Shawn Achor[11] talks about the different impact it can have, depending how you view it. He and his team have found when you perceive stress as a threat, the negative effect it has on your body is significantly increased. However, when you reframe the way you see it – to regard it as a challenge rather than a threat, there's a significant decrease in the negative health effects accompanying the stress. Just changing the story that you tell yourself changes the physical effect stress has on you.

That's potentially massive! (You can see why he called his book 'Big Potential'). The next question is how do you change your story?

Achor argues the starting point is to stop trying to block stress or make it go away. It's there, better to face it. He says a more successful approach is to recognise that its presence indicates something has meaning for you. You wouldn't be feeling like this if you didn't care. The dinner with the in-laws wouldn't stress you if you didn't love your partner and want to make them happy. The presentation at work wouldn't bother you if you didn't care about your job and want to do well. In fact, whatever the situation, somewhere there is a meaning-cue saying, "This is something that matters to me". By then concentrating on the thing that matters, like, "I love my partner, so I want to make this dinner a success", you can channel your stress reaction more positively.

Putting it into practice

The benefits of better stories should be clear to see. In the next chapter we'll look at one of the reasons why some people find this so hard to achieve, and what we can do about it, but before we get to that, it's time for a couple more exercises to help shape the way your stories play out.

Exercise 3.2 – Catch and challenge yourself

This is an ongoing task, so you might need to write it down and remind yourself about it regularly. When you find yourself thinking negatively, consciously challenge those thoughts and reframe them in a more positive or empowering way. For example, if you catch yourself thinking, "I'm terrible at this," reframe it as, "I'm still learning, and I can improve with practice."

Exercise 3.3 – *The A-E model (From Cognitive Behavioural Coaching for Dummies)*[12]

The A-E model is a novel way of forcing yourself to take a different view of events. It builds on the last exercise but takes things a little further. There are five steps, A-E, and you work through each in turn, writing down your answers:

A. Activating situation – what is the situation you're facing?

B. Belief, thought, or expectation – write down what you're thinking about it. Depending on the situation this might be things you believe about yourself, about other people, or about events which might unfold.

C. Consequential action arising from (B) – because you feel that way or hold those beliefs, what does that mean to your life? How is it making you feel? Do you want to feel this way?

D. Disputing the belief – are there other ways to look at this situation which might be more helpful?

E. Exchanging the thought for something else – How would you rather look at this situation? What, more empowering, option is there? How can you reframe this, so you're not left feeling bad?

To put this into an example:

A. I'm overweight and unfit.

B. I've let myself go, my wife always makes a real effort and I look awful. She goes to the gym and runs. I just work and do family stuff.

C. I'm lazy and worthless. It's only a matter of time before she realises and leaves me. I can't stand looking at myself, what kind of role model am I for my son?

D. I work hard and yet I'm still a present and attentive husband and dad. I make a point of always having date night with my wife. She tells me she loves me more than ever. I never miss my son's school events and I love nothing more than playing football with him.

E. I could take steps to improve my fitness. I know I always feel better when I do a bit of cardio and it'll help me kick a ball with my son. It doesn't need to define who I am, it's just a small part of my life I could give a bit more attention.

Now, take one of the situations from exercise 3.2, or reflect on a past experience when you were thinking negatively.

How could you reframe that situation? Use the steps to guide your thinking and help yourself turn it around.

Exercise 3.4 – Be your own friend

This is always a good one to do when you're feeling low about yourself. Step outside the situation and imagine you were talking to a friend instead. If someone you cared about was in the same circumstances, with the exact same conditions, what would you tell them? Would you be able to find a different story to the one you're currently telling yourself?

Exercise 3.5 – Reframing stress

This exercise is one of the simplest in this book, but also one of the most powerful. This might not be something to do now, depending on how you're currently feeling, as you need to have something you're feeling stressed about. If you're currently running along quite happily, you can park this exercise for another time. If, however, there's something causing you stress right now, this is for you.

Take your paper and pen and write a few words describing the thing you're stressed about at the top of the page. Now look at it and ask yourself, "What am I really bothered about? What is the piece that matters to me that's sitting underneath this stress?" Once you've found the underlying reason, write it down, and write it in full. So, if the reason you're stressed about your presentation at work is the fact you really want to impress your boss because you love your job so much and want to do well, write, "I love my job and I really want to do well".

Now you've done that, move your focus to the statement, and away from the presentation. Keep in your mind you love your job, you want to do well, and any feelings of stress you're experiencing are nothing but a perfectly natural series of events, started in your brain, and designed to help you achieve your goals. Your body's trying to assist as you prepare for the presentation in the one way it knows how.

Then, when you feel the adrenaline and cortisol kick in, the heart rate rise, and the butterflies arrive in the tummy, recognise them for what they are – your body's helping hand; preparing you to do your best because you love your job, and you want to do well.

'Too long; didn't read' chapter summary

The brain is an incredibly complex organ, but it needs to take short-cuts to deal with the amount of information in the world around you. These short-cuts, or heuristics, determine the way you see the world and the way you interact with it.

You effectively create complex spam filters which decide what you're going to pay conscious attention to and what you're going to ignore. Once something gets through these filters, you're likely to see much more of it. You see this when you get a new car and suddenly, they appear to be everywhere. This is known as the Baader Meinhof phenomenon (or frequency illusion).

If you want to change your reality and live a happier, more fulfilled life, you need to change some of your shortcuts, so your filters let in more of the things you want and shut out more of the things you don't.

There is a widely used saying – 'neurons which fire together, wire together'. This tells you that the more you think about things, the more set your filters become. If you concentrate on positive things, you're more likely to create positive filters. If you concentrate on negative things, it's more likely your filters will be negative.

The brain loves a story. It's hardwired to respond to one– our ancestors had no other way of passing information down. When things happen, you tend to tell yourself one of two types of stories: positive stories (optimism), or negative stories (pessimism). By changing the nature of the story, you can change the nature of the experience.

One good way to treat a challenge you're facing is to ask yourself three important questions:

1. Is it really happening, or am I imagining it's worse than it is?

2. Can I change it?

3. Can I accept it and make the world a better place despite it?

If it isn't really happening, you can simply re-frame the situation to create a more positive story. If it is happening but you can change it, your story becomes one of how to overcome. If it's real and you can't change it, but you can live with it, you need to develop your internal story to accept it for what it is and move past it.

A key technique for creating better stories is 'reframing'. This comes from the work of Aaron Beck and has been proven to be successful across a range of psychological domains but can be particularly effective when dealing with stress.

By perceiving stress as a positive reaction to events that matter, you can reduce the amount of damage it does to your body.

CHAPTER 4:
IT'S NOT YOUR FAULT

"That's my gift. I let that negativity roll off me like water off a duck's back. If it's not positive, I didn't hear it. If you can overcome that, fights are easy" – George Foreman

"Just because you're paranoid doesn't mean they aren't after you." - Joseph Heller, Catch-22

We're just negative creatures

THE HUMAN BRAIN is a busy little bee, constantly whirring around and popping things into your consciousness all the time. The internet tells us the average human has around 60,000 thoughts every day. Of course, nobody knows exactly how many thoughts you have, and I've never been able to find a source for this claim, but one study in 2020 put forward a seemingly more reasonable estimate of 6,200 thoughts per day[1]. If you're sleeping for eight hours, this means 6,200 thoughts in the remaining 16 hours, at the rate of one every ten seconds or so. (Even the much smaller figure is a lot of thinking). The brain is constantly presenting you with things to occupy your mental resources; What shall we have for tea? Why did he just look at me like that? Who on Earth comes up with the names for colours – I mean, 'cerise'? Come on!

Whether it's 6,000 or 60,000 thoughts going through your brains each day, one thing scientists do seem well agreed upon, is that a significant proportion of those thoughts are repetitive (the same ones you had yesterday) and most of them are negative.

Best estimates suggest around 60% of all the thoughts you have are negative in nature meaning you potentially spend around nine-and-a-half waking hours each day thinking negative thoughts. Wow! No wonder people seem to be stuck in a rut.

The self-help 'industry' will tell you the answer to this is to 'think positively'. Sadly, positive thinking isn't the answer. You can spend as much time as you like trying to fill the gaps between negative thoughts with positive self-affirmations - yes, you are a strong and independent woman, Kevin – but it's like adding water to a cup of rice. It might fill the little gaps, but it won't change the fundamentals of the contents. It's still a cup of rice, it's just soggy rice now.

In this chapter, we'll look at the reasons why we have this tendency toward negativity. We'll also explore some of the good evolutionary reasons for it and start to consider how you can challenge your very nature to help you tell more positive stories by default. Like everything we cover in this book, it isn't an overnight fix. It won't change your world view in one go, but if you do the right things often enough, you can turn the ship around.

The starting point? Knowing why you do it.

Negativity bias

Your 'spam filters' provide you with great assistance in managing the day-to-day tribulations of life. As you saw in the last chapter, your heuristics (short-cuts) make life easier in many circumstances. Unfortunately, they can also make life more difficult when your cognitive biases get in the way. Your interpretation of the world can become skewed, resulting in less desirable results. One of the most important cognitive biases is our negativity bias.

Put simply, negativity bias says you give greater weight of importance to bad events happening around you than to good events. When presented with equal amounts of 'good stuff' and 'bad stuff', it's the bad which will occupy your mind.

If you want proof of this, simply watch the evening news on the TV. Every day, we're presented with almost endless quantities of suffering, misery, and hardship. This doesn't mean there aren't good things going on in the world. For every crazed attack, there are countless acts of generosity and kindness. It's just those events don't make it to the news. Even the 'and finally...' good news story seems to have had its day now. All that's left in most news bulletins is the bad. Why? Because it is what people seek out.

Newspapers are the same. A negative headline sells better than a positive one. A tale of a celebrity doing wrong will see papers fly off the shelf. A tale of the same celebrity donating millions of pounds to help people less fortunate might make it to the middle pages but will probably include an insinuation there was some self-serving reason behind their action.

If you look at personal relationships, when someone you know to be dishonest tells the truth, you tend to treat this as an outlying event – something that might happen occasionally without altering that person's fundamental character. What, then, if someone you believe to be honest is caught telling a lie? Research shows you're much more likely to change your entire opinion about them. Rather than seeing the lie as an outlying event, you're more likely to reclassify that individual in your mind as now being a dishonest person. You give greater weight to the negative, than the positive.

Effectively, people want the misery. They want the bad news and to believe the worst in people. They seek it out, but it doesn't mean they're somehow twisted. In fact, it isn't their fault at all. It's all in the way the brains wired – and for good reason.

Lions and rabbits

Picture the scene: a rabbit is sitting on a stone, eating a rather lovely green leaf for lunch. The sun's beating down and a light wind is blowing through the grass. All is well in our rabbit-friend's world. He's probably making plans for the afternoon – a little trot around the field, a few more leafy treats. It would be rude not to, wouldn't it? Suddenly, there's a loud bang. 'Bugs' looks up, startled. There's no obvious indication of where the sound came from, but he's worried anyway. In fact, probably best to err on the side of caution and scarper. He drops his leaf and heads back to his burrow for shelter - he's not keen on being lunch today.

Three thousand miles away, another animal is also having lunch. This one's a lion. He's sitting on top of a much larger rock, surveying his territory as he munches on his latest kill. His plans for the afternoon are to do much the same as he did this morning – lie here and enjoy the sun. By pure coincidence, there's a loud bang where he is too. Unlike the rabbit, though, he looks up, has a glance around, and goes back to eating.

What was the difference between Bugs and Simba? Well, at the most basic level, it's a matter of their position in the evolutionary pecking order. The lion's an apex predator – he does the eating; he doesn't get eaten. The rabbit, on the other hand, is prey. There are countless creatures who would quite enjoy feasting on him and his brain instinctively knows it. He doesn't need to go to rabbit classes to work out the safest option for him is to scarper when there's a potential threat. Worst case, he's left behind a nice leaf; best case, he's just saved his own life.

In evolutionary terms, people are more rabbit than lion. Whilst we might have evolved the technology to master – and destroy – our environment, we're still made of fairly weak flesh and bones. In a fight with a predator, we'd lose more than we'd win. Everything from a shark to a gorilla, a snake, even a bee, has the power to kill us off. Take away our weapons and we're largely defenceless, and just like the rabbit, our brain knows this.

When our ancestors were evolving, they were at risk of attack from other animals. To survive, they needed to be able to protect themselves. As you saw in the last chapter, the release of stress hormones into the bloodstream when confronted with a threat is designed to prepare the body to either fight or run away. Since any threat might be a tiger, the body prepares for every threat as if it were one. Cortisol pumps into our blood and we get ready to hotfoot it away to safety or, if running isn't an option, to give it all we've got in a fight.

This fight or flight response served our ancestors well because it was combined with a cracking early warning system.

A bit of neuroanatomy

No, don't leave me. I promise I'll keep this brief, but it is important.

There's a part of your brain called the amygdala. Well, more precisely, there are two 'amygdalae', but I don't want to lose the goodwill this section requires, so we'll stick with amygdala. This is part of a system in the brain known as the 'limbic system', and you can see it highlighted in the diagram below along with a couple of other important parts we'll come on to shortly:

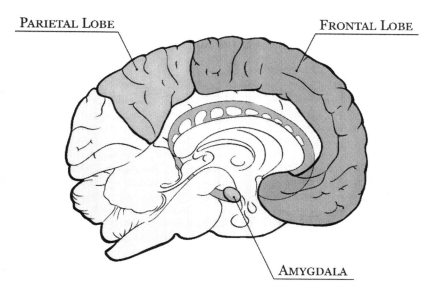

The parts of the brain involved in threat detection.

The limbic system, especially the amygdala, plays an important role in many aspects of human life. It helps with processing of memory and making decisions. It also plays a vital role in our emotional responses – including fear, anxiety, and aggression.

Unfortunately, it's also the amygdala that makes many of those snap decisions we talked about in the last chapter. It's the amygdala that jumps to conclusions and dives in on your behalf based on very little information. This is what Steve Peters calls the 'chimp'[(2)]. Your 'chimp' makes quick judgements with a view to keeping you safe. If someone looks like a threat, this part of the brain won't spend too much time wondering about it, it'll just tell you to scarper like the rabbit - better to be safe than sorry.

Case study 4.1 – The email

OK, well, this wasn't going to be in the book, but events happen around us and life has just presented me with a perfect example of the amygdala in action.

While I was typing out this chapter, an email popped up on the screen in-front of me. I usually turn off my emails when I'm working, but I'd forgotten. The title of this email told me someone had responded to some work I'd put together. Curiosity got the better of me and I opened it – sorry for leaving you for a second.

The person sending the email was disagreeing with my approach. She referenced her own experience and qualifications in a way my amygdala immediately jumped upon. She was attacking me. She was looking to cause trouble for me and was challenging my authority on a particular subject. To my amygdala, she was a tiger, and it was time to fight or run.

My instinctive reaction was to send a 'firm rebuttal', but I didn't. Instead, I took my time and practiced some of the techniques I'll show you later. The tiger soon went away....

Anyway, where were we?

Scientists have estimated as much as two-third of the neurons in the amygdala are devoted to looking for negativity[3]. Given how important your 'chimp' is to your functioning, that's a huge percentage of your resources devoted to looking for 'tigers' in a world where there are relatively few immediate threats to your existence.

You need your amygdala. You certainly don't want to stop it looking after you, but sometimes you might do well to take what it says with a pinch of salt and get some of the other parts of the brain involved before you jump to a decision.

The Dangers of Excessive Negativity Bias

Although there's evolutionary value in looking out for dangers, in today's world where the dangers aren't the same as those faced by our ancestors, there are very real health risks associated with too much focus on the negative.

In The Happiness Advantage[4], Shawn Achor talks about tax auditors. They spend their working days looking for mistakes in their clients' tax returns. All day, every day, looking for mistakes. What do you think happens when they go home? Their kids come home with their school reports, and it isn't the 'A' in English which catches their eye, but the 'C' in Maths. They become wired to negativity. Over time this can have a knock-on effect to their mental health, with higher-than-average incidence of anxiety and depression.

The same is true of lawyers, who are trained to look for the worst-case scenario. Here, Achor reports the incidence of major depressive disorder is 3.6 times greater than it is for the rest of the employed population. That's massive. The nature of the job is potentially contributing to long-term health outcomes by altering the way the brain perceives the wider world.

It isn't just tax auditors and lawyers who suffer, either. All of us are at risk. Remember the stress response in chapter three? If you're exposed to chronic stress, the constant release of cortisol can do huge damage. Being in a constant state of fight or flight readiness can cause increased risk of heart disease, high blood pressure, diabetes, and other physical illnesses. It can weaken your immune system, increase your susceptibility to infection and disease, and slow down the healing process from simple conditions like the common cold. Long term exposure to high levels of cortisol is even associated with osteoporosis and weakened muscles as you age.

As if this weren't bad enough, you're also at risk of mental health issues. Just as lawyers are more likely than average to suffer depression, so people who walk around in a constant state of stress are also more likely to experience mental health issues. Anxiety, depression, and sleep problems are all associated with chronic stress. It can change the way you see the world, bring about a narrower focus, and make your lives generally worse. Not ideal.

We've already looked at some important ways to reframe things for better outcomes, but we can, and probably ought to, do more. There's a stress epidemic happening, and the power to address it lies with each of us – and the other parts of our brain.

Shifting the Focus: Overcoming Negativity Bias

It should be clear you need to guard against letting the amygdala make all the big decisions. It's overly emotional and jumps in with both feet. This is where Steve Peters introduces two other systems within the brain – the 'computer' and the 'human'. It's important to say this distinction between three separate systems in the brain isn't a matter of scientific fact. Rather, it's a way of simplifying the incredibly complex processes going on in the brain at any one point. Since it's a pretty good model, we'll run with it.

The 'human' is the conscious part of the brain - the frontal lobe, or frontal cortex. For the less anatomically minded, this is the front bit of the grey wrinkly part of the brain, shown in the diagram above. This is where you make more logical and analytical decisions, and fewer emotional decisions. This is the part of the brain which will take a step back and consider the best approach to a perceived threat, weighing up possibilities, rather than diving straight in. It can take a considered view on things, looking at all angles and stripping the matter right back to its basic components.

Unfortunately, the frontal cortex is the lazy part of the brain. It spends most of its time doing as little as it can get away with, sitting on the sofa and watching movies. Everything that happens goes through the amygdala first – it acts five times faster than the frontal cortex – and although the frontal cortex knows the amygdala's running around making some odd decisions, most of the time it's happy to let it. What you need to do is force the 'human' element to get involved a bit more. We'll look at a couple of strategies for this shortly.

The third way – the computer

The final 'system' in the brain is what Steve Peters calls the 'computer'. This sits on the top and towards the back of the brain – another part of the grey wrinkly bit, known as the 'parietal lobe'. This is the section which interprets all the information coming from other parts of the brain. It's the quickest of the three operating systems and makes decisions based on rules given to it by both the amygdala and the frontal lobe – the 'chimp' and the 'human'. In other words, this is the automatic spam filter.

Your parietal 'system' contains the core programming which sets your direction. What you hold to be true – your beliefs and your values, along with your mindset, all live there.

If you believe in being honest and kind, this part of the brain will jump on the information it receives from the rest of the brain and marshal your resources to act accordingly. If you believe people are there to be walked over, well, you'll be telling this part of the brain a different story.

Unfortunately, although you start off with a clean slate at birth, you don't only build up useful rules and stories. Sometimes you build up more fundamental issues which need to be resolved. If you want this part of the brain to achieve more positive outcomes for you, you need to give it better programmes to run – you need to tell it better stories. This is something we'll look at in more detail in the next few chapters.

Putting it into practice

As always, we end the chapter with a few exercises for you – this time aimed at keeping the amygdala under control and starting to write better programmes (stories) for the parietal system (the 'computer').

Exercise 4.1 Let it go...

The amygdala is a powerful force in your life. It jumps in to try to protect you, but it's extremely emotional. Sometimes, the most successful way to handle this, is to let it have its moment – but in a controlled environment.

Let's go back to the email example I shared earlier. When the email came into my mailbox, my amygdala started jumping up and down and getting emotional. It saw the content of the email as a personal attack and wanted to fight back. So, I let it. Well, I let it think I did.

I wrote an email telling the sender exactly what I thought. All the reasons why I thought she was a terrible human being and all the reasons why her opinion was both unhelpful and unwanted. I went to town, and then I popped it into my draft email folder and left it there.

By letting my 'chimp' vent in this way, it calmed down. It had its say and let my more rational frontal cortex ('human') get involved. Once the rational part of my brain came to the party, that email was never getting sent, and I deleted it shortly afterwards but, in the moment, it let me get it off my chest and calm down.

This is a technique I use often – vent in a safe environment. It's what my wife calls 'Bruce Willis-ing'. If you've seen the film Pulp Fiction, you'll know there's a scene where Bruce Willis' character has lost a watch which is very important to him, all because his girlfriend forgot to pack it. He goes to his car and, in private, has a 'hissy fit'. He gets it out of his system, and then he cracks on.

Next time you feel your amygdala getting angry, let it have its moment. Give it a safe environment to vent – whether that's sitting in the car and shouting or writing an email for the drafts folder. Just let the chimp have a moan, and you'll find it soon quiets and allows you to move on.

Exercise 4.2 Make a plan

While they may be very different these days, the best way to deal with potential 'tigers' in your daily life, is to have a plan in advance. Write down a list of the things you know 'trigger' your own amygdala into fight mode. It might be tiredness, too much work, particular phrases, it could even be the sound of other people eating (it's an actual thing – called misophonia).

Whatever your triggering events, plan how you'll deal with them. Write down the actions you'll take. For example, you might write, "When my boss dumps more work on my desk and I'm already bogged down, I'll take a five-minute breather, compose myself, and then look at what's the most important work for me to tackle. If I've got too much to do, I'll then go back to my boss and ask which bits she's happy for me to push back for now".

By planning in this way, you're giving your brain the automatic programme to run when confronted with the event. You're putting those programmes into the parietal lobe ('computer'), and remember the parietal lobe acts 20 times faster than the frontal lobe ('human').

Exercise 4.3 Challenging your stories

Once again, we're back to the idea of challenging your internal stories, so this is an exercise to help you do this more effectively. If the parietal lobe's running automatic programmes, you need to think about changing those by telling yourself better stories.

A good way to do this is to concentrate on events which have resulted in filters being wired into your brain – and then systematically rewriting the narrative. This takes time but is so worthwhile. So, where to start? Well, this exercise builds on the introspection (1.1) and belief quadrant (1.2) exercises we did in chapter one, and some of the challenging work we did in chapters two (exercise 2.1) and three (3.2).

The starting point here is to pick an event which left you feeling bad – either with an emotion or an outcome you didn't want. Once again, you're going to step back into the situation and visualise it as clearly as you can. Try to take yourself back to the moment. What were you saying and what were other people saying to you? How did it make you feel? What thoughts were you having? Try to be as clear as you can on those thoughts.

Now ask yourself – did those feelings help me? Did they make me feel better or worse, and did I want to feel that way? If you didn't want them, you've got a story you need to change.

Let's think of an example:

Thought: "I can't ask my clients to pay higher fees… when I tried to position it with a client, I tripped over my words, I made a fool of myself"

If this isn't a feeling you want to have, you need to replace it with a new, more empowering story. You do much more of this in the next chapter, but for now, consider this potential challenge and a replacement story...

Challenges: "What value do I bring to clients? How much money do I make them or save them over the course of the year? Have clients ever told me they didn't think I offered good value? Haven't prices gone up in the general market in the last year? Why wouldn't I also put mine up?"

New story: "I make my clients' lives much better. They love working with me and they get great value for money. Prices rise over time and the increase in my fees is entirely reasonable."

By changing this story and reinforcing it to yourself, next time the fees conversation comes up, it should be a more empowered conversation.

"Too long; didn't read" chapter summary

The human brain is naturally wired to look for negatives rather than positives. Whilst it was nice to notice the good, for our ancestors, it was vital to notice the bad. Walking past a good thing might reduce the amount of happiness they enjoyed, walking past a bad thing might result in them ending up as lunch.

A key part of the brain – the amygdala – is involved in memory, decisions, and emotional responses – including fear and anxiety. It makes very quick decisions without conscious thought but devotes much of its resources to looking for dangers.

Long term over-focus on the negatives can have serious health consequences – potentially increasing incidence of heart disease, high blood pressure, anxiety, depression, and insomnia.

The more you concentrate on dangers around you, the more your brain's processing power will be devoted to looking for them. To overcome this, you need to actively work to change your filters. By changing your internal stories, over time you can rewire the brain to seek out more positives.

You can start to change your world by getting the more conscious part of the brain (the parietal lobe) involved more often, and by putting in place coping strategies for handling the more emotional side of life. The most effective approach is to change some of your automatic processes by rewriting your stories.

CHAPTER 5:
GAME, MINDSET, AND MATCH

"Why, sometimes I've believed as many as six impossible things before breakfast" Lewis Carroll, Through the Looking-Glass.

"Open your mind" Kuato – Total Recall

IF THE PARIETAL system is the fastest part of the brain and it's where your mindset lives, it means your mindset is the first thing controlling your reactions to the world around you. Whatever mindset you've programmed into your brain is acting as the 'first responder' and shaping the way you react, before you've even had time to consciously process events. Your mindset has a massive impact on the way you lead your life. Yet it's something you can change with the right effort, and the importance of mindset is why we're going to devote this chapter to looking at it.

Where do you start?

Let's get one thing on the table straight away. Just as we said at the start of the last chapter, when we talk about mindset, we aren't talking about 'positive thinking'. If only it were so simple. Changing your mindset will naturally result in more positive thinking, but you must do the right things in the right order, and that means consistent and concerted action.

OK so, quick clarifier out of the way, let's talk more about what mindset means.

In simple terms, your mindset is what sets how you see the world around you. It determines whether a given event is perceived as being positive or negative. It's a lens through which you view the world – it's your personal story. Your mindset contains all your attitudes and, as you'll see, it can be a powerful determinant of your life outcomes – even down to your physical and mental health.

The leading voice on this topic is psychologist Carol Dweck. She's one of those people who you've probably never heard of, but whose work is everywhere. If you've heard the term 'growth mindset', you've heard of Dweck's work. In the appropriately titled 'Mindset'[1] (does what it says on the tin), she sets out two categories of mindset: 'fixed' and 'growth'. These two categories are based on the way people perceive ability – do you think we're born with certain levels of ability and intelligence, and that's all there is (fixed), or do you believe, with practice and effort, we can learn to do things and can develop intelligence (growth)?

Life with a growth mindset

According to Dweck, people with a growth mindset believe we're all capable of learning and achieving more. They take the view if they work hard and put in the practice, they can increase their ability and get the hang of things. In other words, they won't say they can't do something, they'll say they can't do it 'yet'. The former closes off the possibility of being able to achieve it, the latter opens the way for a future situation where it is possible.

People with a growth mindset also see setbacks differently – they see them as an opportunity for progression. There's a great quote attributed to Thomas Edison which brings this to life perfectly: "I have not failed; I've successfully found 10,000 ways that won't work". Whether he said it or not, it is a great example of growth mindset in operation. To give you a more modern example which we know is true, the inventor James Dyson tried 5127 prototypes before he finally landed on the right design for his bagless vacuum cleaner! To the growth minded person, each 'failure' takes them one step closer to a success. It's a chance to refine technique, develop new and more creative methods, and to go again.

A good way of thinking about the attitude of someone with a growth mindset is, 'Nothing ventured, nothing gained'. They're much more likely to put themselves out there and try, knowing they'll either succeed or they'll learn – they'll never truly fail.

When people with a growth mindset receive potentially negative feedback, they generally embrace it as a way to learn and to improve. The saying, 'feedback is a gift' resonates with growth minded people, and when they see someone – even a rival – succeed, they're often happy for them. After all, it'll be their time next.

Just thinking about this sounds a more uplifting way to approach life. To come at things with an internal story that separates your worth from your results. Where you'll always have a go and take your chances, even if they don't succeed. Where you can embrace feedback to drive your success further. It all sounds pretty good to me. Besides, what's the alternative?

The fixed mind

According to Dweck, the alternative to the growth mindset is a fixed mindset. These people believe if they can't do something well the first time, they're never going to be able to do it at all, no matter how hard they try. Remember Harriet from chapter one? She was convinced she'd never be able to pass the exams needed to become a financial adviser. Her belief was based on a single past failure. Her fixed mindset was making her believe this one exam was indicative of her overall ability.

Fixed mindset statements are things like, "I can't do maths", or "I'm no good at languages". These sweeping statements are often based on nothing more than the result of one brief attempt (or a single exam result).

To the fixed-minded person, you're born with your list of talents, and these are limited – use them as best you can, because you aren't getting any more! If something falls outside the fixed view of their own beliefs, it isn't worth trying. After all, why set yourself up for failure? If people with a growth mindset think, "Nothing ventured nothing gained", those with a fixed mindset might think, 'Nothing ventured, nothing lost!"

When someone with a fixed mindset suffers a setback, they're much more prone to downing tools and walking away. To them, it just proves they can't do it, and they'll lock away that knowledge to avoid future failure. If they receive negative feedback, it only serves to prove the point and they tend to take it personally. They'll often become highly defensive if the feedback isn't glowing and will generally try to pass the blame on to someone else. They may also become jealous of the person who succeeds rather than be happy for them.

The big problem for these people is the link between their self-view and how other people praise or criticise them. If they receive negative feedback, or see other people doing better than themselves, they're likely to take it as negative reflection of them as a person. Studies have even shown that people with a fixed mindset are more prone to lie about negative outcomes rather than risk being seen in a negative light. In one study, for example, when asked their results, students with a fixed mindset were more inclined to say they passed, even when they failed an exam.

One other finding from Carol Dweck's work was that people significantly misestimate their own ability, but rather than those with a growth mindset overestimating their ability, it was those with the fixed mindset who underestimated their ability – potentially holding themselves back from achieving much more.

This paints a picture of two groups of people walking around like Tigger or Eeyore – either bouncing around in delight or moping around in despondency. The truth is clearly much more nuanced. Dweck points out that rather than being all Tigger or all Eeyore, mindset is a spectrum. You aren't 'growth humans' or 'fixed humans', everyone has traits of each, but you do have dominant mindset characteristics. Importantly, your mindset can be different in response to different circumstances – being more prone to growth in one situation and more fixed in another, as the following example demonstrates:

Case study 5.1 – *The new manager*

A former colleague of mine, we'll call him Jason, was up for his first management role. He called me in a panic. He didn't think he could manage people – he'd never done it before. He watched other managers and believed they possessed natural ability – a natural ability he didn't have. He really wanted the job but was sure he'd fail. It was all making him miserable.

I asked him to peel back the layers and think about what aspects of management he didn't feel he was able to accomplish. He said people wouldn't follow him because he was naturally introverted and didn't have the ability to inspire people. His mindset told him he was never going to be a leader. He kept his head down at work and tried to be invisible. He was what special forces operatives call a 'grey man' – someone who stays in the background and never catches the eye.

We then explored his life outside work. I knew a little about him and I knew he helped with a local football team. I asked him to talk to me about this. He explained it was a youth team for teenage boys in a deprived part of East London. The kids all came from what might be called 'rough' backgrounds. He'd been a member of the team and over time he'd stepped up into a coaching role when his legs stopped wanting to play. He was now the head coach. The lads all called him 'gaffer' and would do anything for him.

When I asked him what his coach role involved, he described, to a tee, the role of a leader. Setting the direction, inspiring everyone, keeping cohesion, and handling issues when they arose. He was already a leader. He'd learned to lead by doing it and had everything he needed right there inside him.

I suggested he frame his answers to the interview questions in terms of his role as team coach, not as team member in his 'day job'. Just a subtle shift in his mindset got him to see a whole world of possibility, and he went on to achieve great things.

Jason clearly had a more growth-oriented mindset when it came to his role with the football club than when it came to his work life. He had higher expectations of himself in football and believed he could achieve more. At work, he had limiting beliefs holding him back. All he needed to do was alter his perception.

The fact Jason was looking at a leadership role also gives us a chance to think about some key aspects of the fixed mindset. As you know, people with a fixed mindset are likely to struggle when they see others doing better than themselves. This often also extends to perception of talent. Many fixed mindset leaders are prone to keeping back talented team members, for fear of being eclipsed, creating a 'negative Pygmalion' or 'Golem' effect for the team member (see chapter two). The manager will create negative environments where the whole team develops fixed mindsets – nobody feels secure, and everyone worries about being judged or treated badly. The dangers of this should be clear, yet it remains all too common in workplaces.

Optimism and pessimism

Martin Seligman[2] – he of the helpless dogs in chapter one – sets out an alternative (albeit similar) approach based on optimism and pessimism.

In his early work (chapter one), Seligman suggested people were more likely to suffer from learned helplessness if they were pessimistic and believed bad events would be: 'pervasive' (having an impact on their wider life); 'permanent' (likely to go on for the long term); and 'personal' (about them rather than the circumstances around them).

Optimistic people, on the other hand, are much more likely to see a way forward, toward a better outcome in the future. These, then, are the one-in-three people who didn't succumb to learned helplessness in Hiroto's human version of the test (the one with the noise that wouldn't stop, just to save you flicking back to chapter one). They were optimistic the music would end in due course and so they took action and didn't give up hope.

Seligman argues 'Pessimism is misery' and those people who score highly on pessimism measures are more likely to:

- Suffer depression,

- Under achieve at work, relative to their ability,

- Have poorer immune functions, and

- Have less pleasure in life.

Yet, it appears many people spend their lives in a perpetual state of pessimism.

Interestingly, Dweck picks up on this idea and points out many people with a fixed mindset aren't pessimists in all circumstances. Often, they seem outwardly positive when things are going well. They're receiving validation and recognition and the world seems rosy. What she's noticed, though, are the difficulties a fixed mindset brings when problems arise.

It's easy to seem positive when you've nothing to worry about - sat on a beach in the sun, with an ice cream and the waves licking at your toes. Only a hardened pessimist (or someone with a severe lactose intolerance) could find anything to feel negative about then. What Dweck studied was how people responded when something went against them, like what happens when the sky turns black, and a jellyfish stings you?

This is the point where those with a fixed mindset cave to pessimism because their view of the world is dependent on constant positive reinforcement from others. Remember Mae from chapter one? She may have seemed incredibly positive when her sales figures were topping the table, but when things turned against her, she reverted to a fixed mindset and started to struggle.

Switching mindset

Dweck and Seligman do agree on one key point – it's possible to change your mindset if you want to. Your mindsets are your beliefs, and your beliefs are your stories. You can learn to be optimistic and can switch toward a more growth-focused worldview. You can reprogram your own mind – and you can do it all from the comfort of your own home, with better stories, told consistently. Such a simple change to your internal story telling can have huge consequences. The more you concentrate on what you can do and the opportunities available to you, the more your brain will come to accept this as your truth. Over time it will change its internal biology – it literally rewires, in a rather grand sounding process called 'neuroplasticity'.

As you've seen, people with a fixed mindset believe their talents are set at birth. In their view, there's no point in trying to learn new skills or to do things better, because whether you can do it or not isn't in your control – it's your innate ability. People with a growth mindset disagree. They believe you can learn new skills if you have the right help and practice and, through neuroplasticity, the scientists have proven this to be true.

In chapter three, we said that 'neurons that fire together, wire together' and this is the basic principle of neuroplasticity. In fact, every time we've talked about story and telling yourself better stories, we've been talking about neuroplasticity.

Correctly defined, neuroplasticity is, "The ability of neural networks in the brain to change through growth and reorganisation". Although this happens at the greatest rate in childhood, it can happen at any point through your life, with conscious effort.

One of the most enlightening studies on neuroplasticity involved analysis of London taxi drivers. This study, conducted by Eleanor Maguire and colleagues[3] looked at the brains of new London taxi drivers as they underwent the lengthy training programme known as 'the knowledge'. For those who don't know, the knowledge is possibly the world's most rigorous test of spatial memory. New taxi drivers must learn the fastest route between any two points based on the time of day, but also need to be able to navigate based on descriptions of places given by passengers. If you jump in a black cab and ask to go to the building with the 'prickly fireball, cactus-type thing on the top', they'll get you to the Great Fire of London monument in the quickest way possible. It's quite a skill! To learn this amount of spatial information takes several years and it provided the perfect opportunity for Maguire and team to demonstrate neuroplasticity in operation. They scanned the brains of the trainees at the outset of their 'knowledge' training, and then again at the end. You can probably guess what they found – the part of the brain involved in spatial memory (known as the hippocampus) had significantly enlarged through the period of training.

What made this test so important was the fact it eliminated any potential element of 'nature over nurture'. If the enlargement was due to natural development, it would have occurred equally in those who were doing 'the knowledge' and those who weren't. The fact it occurred only in the trainee taxi drivers showed neuroplasticity in action.

This study has been taken as offering conclusive proof of our ability to change the way our brain is wired – and other studies have supported its findings. The key takeaway here? If you want to rewire your brain, you need to make consistent and regular effort. This is one of the main reasons why being told to 'adopt a positive mindset' won't cut it. Taxi drivers don't change their brain structure by picking up their black cab and printing a few business cards. They change it through daily practice and work.

There is small health warning – Dweck points to the danger of what she calls a 'false growth mindset'. This happens when someone learns the benefits of a growth mindset and decides they'll adopt one but doesn't make the necessary changes. They end up describing a growth mindset, without changing their personal stories to develop one. Like our taxi drivers jumping in a black cab without doing the work first, it might be OK for a while. The first few fares might be to places they know well. Unfortunately, when someone gets in and wants a more obscure journey, it all goes wrong. The 'false growth' person can get away with it for a short while, but when things go wrong, the fixed mindset comes roaring back, often with the individual in question deciding growth mindsets don't work. To be effective in the long term, neuroplasticity requires constant reinforcement, and we'll look at some helpful techniques for that shortly.

There are always going to be limits to what you can achieve, and nobody is suggesting you can turn yourself into Picasso, Ronaldo, or Stephen Hawking by rewriting your internal stories. Some people do possess incredible skills and some of those skills are beyond what you can be taught. But here's the thing – if Picasso had never picked up a paint brush, Ronaldo had never kicked a football or Stephen Hawking had never pondered questions of physics, they wouldn't have achieved what they did, either. The point Dweck makes is simply: you don't know what you're capable of achieving until you try. If you never put yourself on the line because your fixed mindset tells you you're incapable of achieving anything, you'll never know, and you might just miss out on amazing opportunities.

Case study 5.2 – Sink or Swim

In 2015, I sat with my wife by the side of a swimming pool in Thailand. I told her how annoyed I was that I couldn't swim. I'd never learned as a child, and it was a life skill I felt I should have. Her response? "Well why don't you learn?"

The fixed mindset approach to her question would have been to point out that I was over 40 and had no idea where to start. If I was destined to swim, the lessons I'd been given at school would have done the job. After all, when I was at school, my brain was primed to learn new things. In my 40s, the best days of my athletic ability were long behind me. But I didn't want the fixed mindset. Instead, I thought about ways I could learn now and how I could incentivise myself. I asked friends if anyone knew of an adult swim teacher, and I gave myself a concrete goal by entering a full-distance triathlon. By having a clearly defined target – 7 months to learn to swim and be good enough to get around 2.4 miles in a lake with 3,000 other people – I had something to work to. The swim teacher I picked was the very personification of growth mindset - he believed that anyone could learn at any age.

Sure enough, seven months later I completed Ironman UK. I still describe my swimming style as 'controlled drowning avoidance', and I'm never going to be a front-of-the-pack competitor, but I can swim. Had I let the fixed mindset prevail, I'd have deprived myself of one of the best days of my life.

The power of optimistic growth

If you're open to the idea of change, you're probably already growth-oriented and quite optimistic. If you're naturally more fixed and somewhat pessimistic, you might need an extra incentive to stick with me. Well, here it is… your health might depend upon it.

Let me explain. There's a body of research which shows people with a growth mindset are healthier, happier, and even live longer lives. Research, by Weidong Tao and colleagues, found students with more growth-oriented mindsets suffered significantly lower incidence of mental health problems[4]. This backs up the work of Carol Dweck, who found a higher incidence of depression amongst those with a fixed mindset.

Further research, by Julia Boehm and colleagues[5], found a link between positive psychological wellbeing and lower incidence of coronary heart disease. While Hermioni Amonoo and colleagues found optimism was also linked to lower risk of coronary disease[6]. And these aren't the only studies to show this effect.

The moral? Adopting a more optimistic and growth-oriented approach can lower your chances of a heart attack.

The curse of imposter syndrome

Before we move away from mindset, we need to consider one of the most prevalent ways people are held back by their minds – imposter syndrome. This syndrome (or phenomenon as some prefer to call it) is a psychological situation in which you doubt your own ability, skills, or talents. This happens regardless of the evidence presented. For instance, someone with imposter syndrome may regard themselves as 'blagging it' or feel they're somehow lying to other people, because those people perceive them to be more intelligent or capable than they believe themselves to be.

Feeling like you're somehow cheating the system or holding a position you don't deserve can be incredibly debilitating and research has shown people who experience imposter syndrome may encounter other mental health issues. Worryingly, many people with imposter syndrome may not seek out help for these mental health struggles because they also play down the severity of their own symptoms – "I'm sure other people have it worse than me..."

Recent research by Rebecca Noskeau and colleagues, at the University of Nottingham,[7] has been seeking to understand more about imposter syndrome and found a link between that and fixed mindsets: a fear of failure. People with fixed mindsets don't want to be seen to fail and this fear puts them constantly on guard, waiting to be 'found out'. This research demonstrates that it's possible to reduce or eliminate the effects of imposter syndrome for some people simply by working toward a more 'growth-oriented' mindset.

Yes, but...

I recently read a newspaper article in which the journalist criticised people like me for talking about more positive mindsets, and adopting new approaches, at a time when people are struggling with multiple social challenges. I'm paraphrasing the journalist slightly, but the broad note of her message was, 'a positive mindset won't put food on the table.' OK... a serious point and one deserving of consideration, because to an extent she's right.

As I've said elsewhere, I have no intention of belittling anyone's problems. Some things ARE hard, I know, I've been there myself. Challenges are real - losing your job is devastating, struggling with relationship breakdowns is a truly miserable experience. But I always come back to one thing - if those events are happening, they are outside our control. Just like Viktor Frankl said of his time in Auschwitz, we can't control the events around us, but we CAN control our response – in fact it's the only thing truly within our control.

If you lose your job, you can either approach the fact with a fixed mindset and allow it to knock you down, or you can approach it with a growth mindset and believe there are opportunities for you to develop and that something better will come from it. The objective circumstances don't change, but your internal representations of the circumstances change, your mental health is likely to be better supported, and research shows you're more likely to spot opportunities for your next job and take them.

So, while the journalist was right in saying we can't change the world around us by thinking differently about it, I would argue we can change the effect it has on us and put ourselves in the best possible position to come out of it positively. For me, that makes focusing on mindset a worthwhile endeavour.

Turning the ship

Now you know the benefits of a more growth-oriented internal story, how can you make the shift from a fixed mindset and nurture your new growth mindset? Well, a good starting point is simply reading this chapter. Research has shown simply knowing the difference between a growth and a fixed mindset can start the process of adopting more positive ways of thinking. In other words, when you don't even know there are two different ways of thinking, how can you possibly change from a less empowering mindset to a more empowering one? So, congratulations, you've already started the journey.

The next step is to identify when you're having fixed mind-set thoughts. We'll look at an exercise shortly to consider where these thoughts might come from and pre-empt them, but it's also good to be on the lookout as you go about your daily life.

When something happens, pause, and consider whether you're looking at the event with a growth or a fixed mindset. You know from chapter four, pausing helps give you time to control your amygdala, so it's going to serve a double benefit. As well as allowing you to be less emotional in your reactions, it gives a chance to ask yourself some key questions:

- Am I open to possibility?

- Have I separated the event from who I am as a person, or am I linking the event to my personal worth and creating an internal story which somehow diminishes me?

You can also improve your chances by creating the best environment for success. Simply committing to action isn't enough to bring about lasting change. You need a specific plan of action. The more detailed this plan is, the more chance you have of following through with it. For instance, if you want to improve your fitness, that would be a good area for a growth mindset. The more growth-oriented you are, the more you'll be telling your brain to accept the possibility of improved fitness, and to look for ways to make that change. Unfortunately, without giving the brain a specific roadmap, it's likely to be left looking but not knowing how to act.

If, however, you commit to a particular plan, such as: "Tomorrow morning, I'll get up at 6.30am, have a quick cup of coffee and leave the house at 7.00am to head to the gym. I'll run 5km on the treadmill and then swim 20 lengths of the pool. Once I've done that, I'll treat myself to ten minutes in the steam room", well, now you've a concrete plan the brain can get right behind. (You've even built in some reward!)

This speaks to another important part of the growth mindset - it's a reward for effort, not talent. The reward isn't linked to running at a specific pace, or completing the swim in a certain time, it is a reward for following through on your plan. When you reward outcomes only, you create greater pressure on yourself to achieve results, and you foster the fixed mindset. If you only reward yourself when you hit certain metrics, you're more likely to regard yourself as having 'failed' when you have a bad day. Instead, by rewarding the effort, you're more likely to continue to do so, which leads to improvements over time

It might sound like a small thing, but people with a fixed mindset are constantly on the lookout for the dopamine hit which comes from being told they've done a good job.

Picture yourself putting a post on your favourite social media platform. How long do you give it before you're checking to see if you've had any reactions? How do you feel if you don't get any likes? People with a growth mindset might still enjoy the recognition, but they recognise it's the effort they put in which drives the results. They don't constantly look for the validation, they just trust the process. If people react to their posts, great. If they don't, so be it.

It's important to remember you can't change everything. I don't like black olives or anchovies and nothing you can do is going to alter that situation. I'll never understand how anyone could like them. Little hairy fish? What is wrong with you people? I could put in as much mindset work as I like, and they'd still repulse me. But that's OK, not everything needs to be changed. I can live my life quite happily without eating the furry fish or the olives. The areas *I* need to concentrate on are the ones causing me pain in my life.

In chapter three, Mo Gawdat's model offered a way to help you consider the problems in your own life – Is it real? Can I change it? Can I live with it and make the world better despite it? The areas you want to change with a more powerful mindset are the second and third groups – those which are both real and which you can either change or learn to live with.

Setbacks

Like any great endeavour, setbacks are going to happen. Even Carol Dweck, the original creator of the 'growth mindset' concept, admits she has setbacks from time to time. Her natural 'wiring' is for a fixed mindset, and she has to work to maintain the growth approach.

I'm the same. I'm very open about the troubles I had as a younger man. Adopting a growth mindset has taken time and effort, and sometimes I slip. Some days I don't feel positive, some days I don't see the opportunity, and some days a piece of feedback is more likely to be taken as a personal attack than an opportunity to make things better. What's important is recognising this as a perfectly normal part of life.

Adopting a growth mindset is not like putting on a new suit of clothes – it takes work and time. Slips are normal and perfectly OK. What matters is how you respond to those setbacks. If you recognise them for what they are – temporary and passing – you can reset and move on again. Remember Seligman's three areas for learned helplessness – the slip isn't permanent, it isn't personal, and it isn't pervasive. It doesn't reflect who you are as a person. Keep those facts in mind and you'll stay on top of things.

In fact, you can even make those slips opportunities for growth. By spotting which circumstances are most likely to make you revert to a fixed mindset, you can more easily guard against them. In my case, I know I'm more likely to slip when I'm tired. That knowledge allows me to be more conscious of my mindset whenever I'm lacking sleep – if I've got to collect feedback on my work, I'm having a nap first!

Putting it into practice

As we move to the next chapter, we'll look at a way to supercharge your mindset and amplify the benefits of the work you've done so far. Before we get to that though, to round off this chapter, here are a few exercises to help you to develop more empowering growth-based internal stories.

Exercise 5.1 - *The third person*

Your own issues feel pressing and immediate. When you talk to others about their issues, it's easier to look at their problems more dispassionately and with greater detachment. This exercise helps you to look at your own problems in the same way, moving from the fixed mindset toward a more growth version.

All you need to do is consider a current issue causing you stress or angst. Then write about it in the third person. If I'm currently worrying about a presentation I've got to give, I might write:

"Jon is worrying about giving a presentation at work. He thinks his colleagues will be judging him and wondering why he's been asked to do this piece of work".

Once you've done that, finish the story by looking at the problem with the outside perspective. Search for the alternative view:

"Jon has been asked to do this presentation because he's been involved in the project. Everyone knows he's been working

Rewritten

on this for months and they've all seen him putting in the hard work. It is highly unlikely anyone will be judging him, but rather they'll see him as someone with inside understanding of the issues involved".

Exercise 5.2 – Feedback please

You may see this one as a bold move, but it's well worth trying. Find someone you trust, who you know has your best interests at heart ideally a friend rather than a partner or family member (they're too close to you).

Then, actively seek out constructive feedback from them on a particular area of your life. When they give it, don't respond. (You can thank them; you're not rude. Just don't discuss or debate the feedback). Instead, pause, and reflect on what you've been told.

If you're naturally prone to a fixed mindset, you're more likely to experience your amygdala firing up ready to fight or run, which is why it's so helpful to use someone you trust. Instead, take a deep breath, and ask yourself, "What can I learn from this?" Even taking this simple step begins the process of creating a new story for the brain, and with practice, it can become your default position.

Exercise 5.3 – Screw it, let's do it…

Richard Branson, founder of the Virgin Group, has a philosophy which is very much one of a growth mindset – 'let's have a go and see what happens'. If it works, great. If it doesn't, try another way. (He even wrote a book about his experiences of setting up Virgin, called 'Screw it, let's do it').

This exercise is about you doing the same – on your own scale. Ask yourself if there's something you've been putting off for some time. Something you've wanted to try, but you've let your mind talk you out of it.

Now think about what you can do, today, to make that thought a reality. How can you take a positive step toward doing it? You may find giving yourself a target to work toward is enough to switch your mindset from inaction to action, just as it was for me with swimming.

Exercise 5.4 – A concrete and vivid plan

As you know, wishful thinking isn't going to change your mindset. Instead, you need to make a vivid and concrete plan and then visualise it happening. This means sitting down with a pen and paper (or laptop) and considering the ways you currently employ a fixed mindset.

Look at yourself in the following areas:

- Taking opportunities

- Handling setbacks

- Responding to feedback

- Hearing of other people's success (especially when you're struggling)

Now, for each of these, think about how you can replace your limiting fixed mindset approach with a more empowering growth mindset. When you're presented with feedback, for instance, and you recognise the usual sinking feeling in your stomach and your amygdala firing up, how would you rather respond? What would be the 'growth' approach to take? Once you know what your approach would look like, vividly imagine yourself in that situation. Picture yourself responding to the event in that way.

Through continuously practising this technique, you can start to rewrite your automatic internal stories toward your desired approach. Importantly, by having this concrete idea of your growth plan, even when you're derailed you have a place to which you can reset, and that makes it more likely you'll succeed in the long run.

'Too long; didn't read' chapter summary

Your mindset is how you see the world and how you interpret the events which take place within it. It's a collection of your attitudes, and a powerful determinant of your outcomes.

Psychologist, Carol Dweck, categorises mindset into 'growth' and 'fixed' versions. People with a growth mindset believe we're all capable of learning and achieving more. They take setbacks as opportunities for progression and see feedback as a way to improve. When someone else succeeds, they're typically happy for them.

People with a fixed mindset believe you're either born with skills or you aren't – your 'lot' is set at birth. When they have a setback, they take this as evidence they can't do something. When they get feedback, they see it as criticism. They're more likely to be jealous than happy for the other person who succeeds.

Rather than being binary, these mindsets are on a spectrum. We all have traits of each, and your mindset can be different in response to different circumstances – being more prone to growth in some cases and fixed in others.

An alternative approach proposed by Martin Seligman uses the terms optimist and pessimist, and suggests optimistic people tend to be less bogged down by learned helplessness and less held back by negative beliefs.

Importantly, both Seligman and Dweck agree it's possible to change your mindset. You can reprogram your individual mindset to be more optimistic, more growth focused. Beliefs are core to your mindset, they're the stories you tell yourself. If you change your stories, you change your mindset.

Research shows you can alter the biology of the brain – a process known as neuroplasticity – by changing the way you think. Concentrating on things in a repeated and conscious fashion encourages your brain to form new neural connections, effectively creating new hard-wired stories.

You can't necessarily turn yourself into a world-famous scientist or composer by changing your mindset but, equally, you have no way of knowing the extent of your ability if you never put it to the test.

As well as the benefits to your potential life outcomes, many studies have shown improved health outcomes associated with a more growth-oriented mindset. Other research has shown growth-minded people are less likely to suffer imposter syndrome.

The process of changing mindset isn't instant – it isn't like taking off one set of clothes and putting on another, but with work and patience it is achievable. This doesn't mean you'll never experience setbacks, but it will become easier to revert to a growth mindset as you become more experienced in living that way.

CHAPTER 6:
THE POWER OF GRATITUDE AND MINDFULNESS

"As we express our gratitude, we must never forget that the highest appreciation is not to utter words, but to live by them." – *John F. Kennedy*

"Yeah, cheers, thanks a lot" – *Patsy Stone, Absolutely Fabulous*

Reasons to be cheerful...

IN RECENT YEARS, a whole new area of human performance improvement techniques has emerged, focussed on the power of two important things: gratitude and mindfulness. You might think that sounds a bit like hippy tree hugging but stick with me because the results are astonishing. The simple act of focusing on and appreciating the positive things in life, and paying attention to the here and now, can significantly increase resilience and reduce the effects of learned helplessness. In other words, they can help you rewrite your internal stories to focus positively on the things you already have, rather than always looking at the things you don't.

I first stumbled across this research when I read a book called The Resilience Project, by Hugh Van Cuylenburg[1]. The author is an Australian who travelled to India to teach local children. These children were poor in the most literal sense of the word, they had nothing. Yet he found them to be happy and contented. Why, he wondered, did he feel so lacking when he had so much if they felt happy when they had so little?

What he discovered was gratitude and mindfulness. These children who had nothing, appreciated everything. Every small detail around them gave them a possibility for joy and they lived constantly in the present moment. They didn't focus on the struggles of their past or the potential troubles of their future.

One child walked around constantly pointing and saying, 'This', as he found something he was grateful for. It might be the sun in the sky, the way the leaves rustled on the trees, the laughter of a friend. His brain had been wired to look for the small pleasures in his life that made each day unique. When he saw them, he called them out, further reinforcing the message for his brain – 'This is something good, find me more'.

Now cut back to busy life in a UK or American city. The hustle culture. Everybody walking along at fast pace, pushing each other out of the way to get to the train. All so they can get to their desk quicker and sit there for 10 hours or more, before turning around and coming back the other way. When they arrive home, they're exhausted, eating dinner whilst watching the TV, not tasting the food they put in their mouths, simply refuelling. Then sleep, rinse, and repeat. They live in one of the richest countries on Earth, at the richest time in human existence and they appreciate, well, not much of it.

I encountered Van Cuylenburg's work at just the right time – during the first Covid lock-down. I was forced to sit still. My clients had cancelled all my projects, so there wasn't much choice, but the lockdown coincided with a period of lovely weather. I sat in my garden, listening to the sounds of nature starting to creep back into the world around me, as confidence built in the animal kingdom in response to the retreat of humankind. I took on the approach of the small boy. I resolved to find things each day that I was grateful for and, however stupid I felt, I'd point at it and say, "This". Gratitude is simply that – it's about appreciating the things you have, rather than worrying about the things you don't.

Although it might sound a bit 'out there', this approach is backed by good science. Our old friend, Martin Seligman (of learned helplessness in chapter one and optimism/pessimism in chapter five), found when they spent time at the end of each day writing down three things for which they were grateful, his participants' overall levels of happiness and satisfaction increased. The simple act of looking for the positives in their lives made them more positive overall. The longer they did this, the better things got. Happiness scores increased and depression scores decreased[2].

Neuroscientists have confirmed this using brain scans. Prathik Kini and colleagues, at Indiana University, found when participants completed a daily gratitude journal, neural changes took place which were associated with, "significantly greater and lasting neural sensitivity to gratitude". In other words, the more gratitude participants showed, the more things they found for which they could be grateful[3] – These participants demonstrated neuroplasticity and better internal stories just by showing gratitude.

And there's plenty more research where that came from. I won't hit you with all of it but, suffice to say, many different studies have confirmed the same findings. Gratitude improves outcomes – everything from recovery from heart attack[4], through better mental health[5] and even calming the overactive amygdala (your chimp from chapter four)[6].

By spending time each day looking for things to be grateful for, you can change for the better the way your brain is wired. I've done this myself and I'm a walking case study for the power of it...

Case study 6.1 – Kilimanjaro, twice

I love mountains, always have. So, I was always going to go to Kilimanjaro. It's the tallest free-standing mountain on Earth, and the highest place on Earth you can walk to – no ropes or ladders needed. At nearly 6,000m above sea level, it towers above the Tanzanian plain - and it's stunning.

Having looked forward to the trek for years, when I got with-in a few hours of the summit, only to have to turn back due to severe altitude sickness (coughing up blood really is no fun) I was initially devastated. My whole family knew I was there, I was going to go home a failure, and I had a nine-hour hike back to safety feeling like death-warmed-up to contemplate being one.

But then I changed my viewpoint. I was given three reasons to be grateful.

Firstly, because I was walking back with just one guide rather than my full party of 30, the local wildlife wasn't scared. About two hours from the end of the trek, we encountered a troop of baboons, in-cluding some very young babies. They were crossing the path no more than 50 metres in front of us. We stood and watched these amazing animals as they went about their daily business. I was treated to na-ture at its most beautiful. I'd never have experienced that otherwise, but it's something I'll never forget. One point for gratitude.

The second 'win' came while we were waiting for the taxi. Some local children were walking home from school. In one of the most deprived that areas I've ever been, these three children were dressed immaculately in bright red school jumpers. They stopped to chat with my guide, and I took the chance to ask some questions. They told me how much they loved school, and how lucky they felt to have the opportunity to go. They got up early and walked long dis-tances, just to be able to take up the chance of schooling. It was a real privilege to talk to them and share in their joy. Gratitude two-nil.

The third win came when we got back to the hotel where I'd be staying until my fellow climbers returned. The owner of the hotel brought me coffee in a silver cafetiere. It was the best coffee I'd ever tasted and when I asked him where he got it, he pointed out the window to the coffee growing behind the hotel. 'There', he said. Game, set, and match gratitude.

What could have been an horrendous experience, forever associated with failure, gave me three of the most powerfully positive memories I hold. And when I went back to Tanzania four months later and summited the mountain, it was even sweeter for the experience of the first time.

The view from the top of Kilimanjaro is stunning – you can see the curvature of the Earth (sorry flat Earthers)

The Power of Mindfulness

One of the benefits of practising gratitude is the way it forces you to slow down and look at the world around you. Over time, a lens of gratitude helps you move more towards living in the moment, embracing your blessings as they arise. This deliberate and attentive way of interacting with the world also forms the essence of another positive practice – mindfulness.

Just as practising gratitude develops your mindset by focusing the mind on the good around you, so mindfulness helps develop greater wellbeing by making you more grounded in the present moment.

For some people, this is all a bit too much. I get it. It sounds very spiritual, but when you start to examine it in more detail, the benefits are so powerful. Leaving mindfulness out of this book would have been doing you a disservice.

So, what do we mean by mindfulness? Is it the same as meditation? Well, not quite. Although it is associated with Buddhist meditation, it's been used by many different cultures throughout history. In recent years it's made its way into mainstream psychology; such is the strength of the mental health benefit – just Google the term 'mindfulness-based therapies.' At the time of writing (July 2023) this yielded around 11.8 million search results (in 0.4 seconds too, isn't Google clever?) It's also been the subject for hundreds of articles and research papers in the field of psychology. There's no doubt mindfulness is now part of the fabric of mental health practice.

At its simplest level, mindfulness is about nothing more than focusing all your attention on the moment you're in. To give a more scientific description, it's:

> the awareness that arises out of intentionally attending in an open and discerning way to whatever is arising in the present moment[7].

It's quite easy to get very philosophical at this point. The past is gone, it lives on only in our memories and you've seen already how open to interpretation some of those memories can be. The future has yet to happen, and you've seen the dangers of dwelling too much on what might or might not happen, creating catastrophes or self-fulfilling prophecies. The only thing that exists is the here and now. The exact moment you're in is the only moment available to you – so shouldn't you make the most of it?

England Rugby Union legend Jonny Wilkinson describes his approach to being present as being, 'all of me, in every moment'. He describes doing the washing up as being as important and as powerful for him as scoring the drop-goal that won the world cup. Wilkinson is a follower of the work of a man called Eckhart Tolle[8], who says we spend too much of our lives living in the past or an imagined future. Instead, we need to focus more on the moment we're in and need to break some of the internal stories we tell ourselves, if we're to make the most of the life we have. Sound familiar? (We'll come back to some ways you can develop greater mindfulness, shortly).

The Ripple Effect of Gratitude and Mindfulness

The beauty of working on both gratitude and mindfulness is they create a ripple which can improve many aspects of your life. By actively concentrating on the things for which you're grateful, you develop what's called an 'attitude of gratitude'. In doing so you become more aware of the things other people do for you and the support they show you. Expressing gratitude to people for their help not only improves the strength of the relationship you share with them, but also makes them feel better, increasing their own gratitude and altering their expectations. (Remember the Pygmalion effect in chapter two?)

By showing gratitude, you can create new expectations in people around you and alter their reality. They in turn have the power to improve someone else's life, and so it rolls on. Just as the 'butterfly effect' says the flap of a butterfly's wings on one side of the world can lead to a tornado on the other side of the world, so the expression of gratitude to one person can lead to positive outcomes for someone you may never meet.

Mindfulness shares similar 'ripple effects.' Since being mindful means being present in the current moment, without judgement, it can help you to develop a better and deeper understanding of yourself and the world around you. By having greater self-awareness, we often approach situations with more clarity and greater compassion, again positively impacting our relationships. Mindful interactions with other people are more present, more connected, and operate on a deeper level. When you pay attention to the other person more fully, this in turn can influence them to do the same.

As if this weren't enough, when you combine gratitude and mindfulness together, the result is more than the sum of its parts.

Mindfulness makes you more aware of the present moment, and gratitude practice strengthens your mindfulness practice by helping you focus not just on the now, but on the good things which live in it. People who fully adopt these two practices are more positive, kinder, and more accepting of others, which in turn encourages others to follow suit. And I think that's reason to celebrate!

Case study 6.2 – The Mindful Chef.

A coaching client who works as a sous chef in a busy London restaurant was struggling with the pressure involved in the job. I've never worked in a kitchen, but I've watched Gordon Ramsay on the TV, and talking to this client – who we'll call Kim – I was struck by how her description of her daily work sounded just like it appears on the screen.

"The kitchen," she said, "is a high-intensity environment. Everything needs to be perfect, all the time". Her boss, much like Gordon Ramsay, has a philosophy of 'keep the mistakes in the kitchen', nothing less than perfect food leaves the pass. Imagine that, over and over again. Each meal leaving the kitchen needs to be spot-on, and as second-in-command, the head chef is looking to Kim to make sure the standard is maintained. Her job is effectively to supervise all the other kitchen staff.

Given that intensity, and the expectation that comes with it, it was hardly surprising Kim was feeling the pressure. "I just feel on edge all the time. The job is so stressful and when I get home I'm still wired. I've no chance of unwinding. I'm like a coiled spring."

We spent some time working through some mindfulness exercises – quick and effective breath-based activities, which she could do in the brief breaks she takes at work, along with longer work she could do at home following a long shift.

I followed up with her a few weeks later and she'd been regularly and consistently practising. She told me the exercises helped to ground her in the moment and allow her to focus her attention more clearly on the tasks in hand. Instead of feeling her head was 'stuffed full of cotton wool', she'd developed greater clarity and felt more in control. When she was at home, the longer mindfulness sessions were allowing her to disconnect work and home life and helping her to relax.

Mindfulness was working well for Kim, and she's told me she'll keep up her practice going forward – but I still don't fancy her job!

Putting it into practice

There are many ways you can employ greater gratitude and mindfulness practice every day. We're going to work through just a few of them here, but if you find it works for you, you might want to investigate some more in-depth approaches. Equally, if you aren't sure where to look next, feel free to get in touch and I will happily point you in the right direction.

Exercise 6.1 – Gratitude journaling

Given the amount of research on the power of gratitude journaling, it would be silly not to include this one up front, and it couldn't be simpler. All you need to do is take five minutes at the end of each day to write down three things you're grateful for. That's it.

You should look for different things each time, wherever possible, as the act of looking reinforces your internal filters and encourages your brain to seek more positives.

Initially do this for 30 days and then consider how you feel at the end. Are you noticing more positives naturally? Do you feel better? To help you get in the habit, if you need to, set a daily reminder on your phone and put your notebook and pen near your sofa or bed (wherever you'll be when you write).

Exercise 6.2 – being mindful

There are hundreds of different mindfulness exercises available, but let's start with two: one to do when you're short of time, much like Kim in the kitchen, and another when you have longer.

a) Short on time

Find somewhere you won't be disturbed for a few minutes – an office, a park bench, even the toilet at a push (although the latter might make for some less pleasant breathing exercises)! Sit with your back upright and relax your shoulders. Keep your feet flat on the floor and rest your hands on your lap. If you want to, close your eyes. Then breathe in through your nose for a count of five, hold the breath for a count of six and breathe out through your mouth, for a further count of seven.

Focus your attention on your breath coming into, and going out of, your body. Notice the sensations in your nose as you breathe in, and your mouth as you breathe out. It's quite normal for thoughts to drift into your mind as you do this. Don't worry. Just recognise the thought is there, don't try to avoid it, then return your concentration to your breathing.

This exercise doesn't need to take long. Five minutes is usually enough to restore some clarity to your mind.

b) Going further

When you've got a bit more time, my favourite longer mindfulness exercise is the 'body scan'. The principles are similar to the exercise above, but with this one you can take longer and really settle into it.

You may prefer to do this one lying down either on the bed or a sofa, though the floor will work for some). Find a position that's comfortable – on your side, your back, whatever works best for you.

Now, close your eyes and once again concentrate on your breathing. For three or four minutes, just breathe in through your nose and out through your mouth. Concentrate on the breath. Don't worry about any thoughts popping into your head – just say to yourself, "Thinking", and return your attention to your breathing.

After few minutes, start the body scan. Pay attention to each part of your body, starting at your toes and working up to your head. Notice how each part feels and try to relax it. Once you've done your feet, move up to your calves, your knees, and so on. Don't rush it, the point of the exercise is to pay full attention to each part of the body. To be fully in the moment.

I usually spend ten minutes or so on the body scan and then another ten minutes or so returning my attention to my breath. By the time I'm finished I feel refreshed and clear headed. Give it a go.

Exercise 6.3 – app it

One of the best 'quick fixes' for mindfulness is to use one of the many apps now available on the market. You could try 'Calm',

'Headspace', 'Balance' or something else. You can generally get a free pass to try them for a week or so. Why not download one or two and give them a go. Use some of the guided mindfulness exercises, or just the exercises for getting better, and deeper, sleep. See which works best for you.

While it might not be scientific, I recently tested the Calm app on myself, using their guided sleep meditation every night. My average sleep heart rate fell by two beats per minute over one week. That'll do me.

"Too long; didn't read' chapter summary

Research has shown the act of expressing gratitude can improve your mental health. People who write down just three things for which they were grateful at the end of each day have been found to increase their levels of happiness and decrease their levels of depression.

By looking at things you're grateful for, you're changing the filters you give your brain. You're encouraging it to look for the positives in each situation, rather than dwelling on the negatives. This will help you to overcome your negativity bias.

Mindfulness is a second useful tool. It simply means paying attention to the present moment in an open and non-judgemental way. Although originally associated with Buddhist meditation, mindfulness is now part of mainstream psychology. There are hundreds of research papers all demonstrating significant benefits to the mental health of practitioners. Anyone can practice mindfulness at any point, and there are some excellent apps you can download to your phone to help get you started.

CHAPTER 7:
MAKING IT HAPPEN

"If you want to live a happy life, tie it to a goal, not to people or things." —*Albert Einstein*

"Do it, do it now!" Arnold Schwarzenegger – Predator

AT THE START of this book, I asked you to open your mind and prepare to look at your life in a different way. To take a trip that would set you on the path to a happier and more fulfilled life. Over the course of the last six chapters, we've looked at the power of your mindset and the stories you tell yourself. We've run through various exercises to help you get under the cover of your own mindset and begin the process of change. And this final chapter is all about taking purposeful action. The action you can take to bring about more happiness and success in your life and, as you'd expect by now, it's all based on proven research. Let's dive in.

Getting what you want

One of the reasons people fail to achieve their goals and live the life they want, is because they don't take the time to define what those goals or that life looks like.

Think back to your brain's filters. Your busy mind is constantly sifting through millions of items of 'stuff' in the world around you. The filters determine what gets through and what doesn't. The problem is, if you don't tell the brain about the goal, the filters are more likely to walk past things which could help you move toward it.

Some people talk about 'manifesting'. This is the notion that when you put your goals out into the universe, through some strange cosmic re-ordering and quantum physics, the universe responds to deliver the things you asked for. It probably won't surprise you to hear I think it's nonsense. The idea you emit certain 'vibrations' which attract the things you've asked for through physics just sounds like tosh to me. "Sure, Jackie, I'll ask for a new car, and I'll start vibrating at Lamborghini cadence. I'll be driving a sports car in a matter of days". That said, I do believe there's something going on behind the manifesting phenomenon, and to me it's all about filters.

When 'manifesters' tell the universe what's on their wish list, they're creating new filters – telling new stories. They're telling the brain to be on the lookout for certain things, and the brain responds. When an opportunity comes along, they seize it. Just like the Baader Meinhof phenomenon (chapter three), they're not creating new opportunities, just noticing ones that were there all along. All you need to do, then, is clearly define what you want and give your brain the opportunity to help find those chances. But how do you do that? Well, you can start with 'Why'.

What's your Why?

Unless you've had your head in the sand for the last ten years or so, you've almost certainly heard of Simon Sinek and his TED Talk on 'finding your Why'. If you've not heard of it, it is a good watch – I recommend it. This talk, and his associated books, can be distilled down (with apologies to Simon) into the words of the eminent philosopher Friedrich Nietzsche. He said, "He who has a why to live for can bear almost any how". This concept also echoes back to the example of Viktor Frankl from chapter three. Frankl had a reason to keep going – in his case to help other people – which allowed him to endure unbelievable suffering with a positive mindset.

What Sinek argues[1] is that people spend too long thinking about what they do and how they do it, but don't think enough about the reasons they're doing it – their 'Why'. To give you a good example, when Sam Walton set up Walmart in 1950, he did so with a clear 'Why'. His goal was to serve the people of his local area and to look after them. He believed that if you look after people, they'll look after you. His objective was to help, not to make profit. Profit, he believed, would come from doing the right things. The business bearing his name went on to become a billion-dollar company based on those principles and only struggled when those leaders who followed him began to put profit motives ahead of the original 'Why'.

You can take this idea and translate it into your personal life by looking at your own 'Why'. What is your bigger purpose? If you see your purpose as being to make money, you're much more likely to live unfulfilled lives – after all, how much is enough? Instead, it's about giving yourself a deeper insight into who you are as a person. To think about the reasons why you get up in the morning.

You might think of this as being the core process at the heart of your mindset – the compass by which your inner computer (the parietal part of the brain from chapter four) – will navigate the waters of your life. Read the example below, to see how this works practically:

Case study 7.1 – Improving fitness for the world

I've recently been coaching a client, who we'll call Callie. Within the first five minutes of our conversation, I could see Callie was in a rut. Her problem was motivation.

"I left my job in marketing to set up my own business as a personal trainer. I'd already lined up a couple of clients and I've

picked up a couple more, but I'm not getting the traction I'd hoped. I'm not earning enough to pay my bills and I'm really worried I've made a terrible mistake".

It was quite clear Callie loved personal training, but she was starting to question whether she might have to go back to her marketing career. I asked her to describe where she was right now.

"It's all stressing me out. I'm not concentrating on my clients properly because I'm too busy worrying I don't have enough of them. It's stupid. I'm letting down the clients I do have, worrying about where I can get more! Maybe I'm just not cut out for running my own business after all."

After exploring this in more detail, I asked Callie to tell me why she'd left her marketing job in the first place. What was it that made her make the jump to personal training? Her eyes lit up. "I'm super-passionate about fitness," she told me, "I used to be a bigger girl, I found it hard to keep fit. I could barely get up a flight of stairs without getting out of breath. I'd spend all night on the sofa binge watching bad TV and eating takeaways. I was miserable all the time. Now I'm in good shape, I feel so much better. I just want to help other people get the same results."

We then went through an exercise of breaking down her 'Why' and it boiled down to a very simple life goal – she wanted to help people in her local area live better, and healthier lives, through improved fitness. That was it. Her reason for getting out of bed in the morning. The main problem was she'd lost sight of this because of her slow start.

When we explored her financial situation, she came to see she wasn't as far away from being financially secure as she thought. Just three more clients would mean she could meet her financial commitments and she'd still have plenty of time to find further clients which, as a trained marketer, she knew how to do. She'd just been beaten down by her internal story.

By focusing her attention on the bigger picture – her 'Why' - she cleared some of the fog and set about the task with renewed enthusiasm. She's still personal training and making lives better.

In the introduction to this book, I mentioned my own 'Why', and the 'Why' of my businesses: 'to help ordinary people achieve extraordinary things'. My wife and I run a group of businesses. We want to make profit. But when a decision needs to be made, we come back to our guiding light every time – is this going to help ordinary people do extraordinary things?

If it won't help people develop, achieve more, or live a better and happier life, it probably isn't something we want to get involved with. We've been in business since 2006 and our 'Why' has stood us in good stead all this time.

The key to finding your own 'Why' is to make sure it is fully aligned with your own values and passions. It has to be something which goes beyond the material and beyond you, but which is aligned with who you are (and it isn't always easy to identify). Here, the Japanese have some help to offer.

Learning from Japan – Ikigai

The island of Okinawa is one of the world's so-called 'blue zones.' These are areas of the world where people have the longest life expectancy, with many people reaching the milestone of living for 100 years. Hardly surprising, then, that researchers have been fascinated to explore what makes these people live so long, so we might be able to follow in their footsteps.

Hector Garcia and Francesc Miralles[2] set out to explore the Okinawan secret to long life and what they discovered was the principle of Ikigai. This is the idea that people live longer when they have a purpose, something to make life worth living. In other words, when they have a 'Why'.

Where the work of Garcia and Miralles is particularly helpful, is in breaking down this purpose into four constituent elements. Ikigai, they argue, is found when we are doing work which meets four criteria:

- Something we enjoy doing,

- Something the world needs,

- Something we're good at, and

- Something from which we can earn money.

Ikigai – where the four elements meet, lies our personal meaning.

If you're doing something you're good at and which you love, it's a passion project. If you love it and the world needs it, it's your mission. If the world needs it and you can earn money from it, it becomes a vocation; and if you can be paid for it and you're good at it, it's a profession. The magic happens where all four elements overlap. When you can tick all four boxes at the same time, that's your Ikigai, and pursuing that activity can enhance and extend your life.

You won't always be able to find the one thing that sits across all four categories, but if you're doing something the world needs, you love, and you're good at, sometimes that gives you the strength to carry on earning your living elsewhere and still be happy.

Good goals

To have successful action, there's no getting away from the need for goals. (I know, I can hear you groaning from here). Any search of goal setting online will produce countless references to either the 1953 Yale Study or the 1959 Harvard study of goal setting. In each case, so the story goes, students who wrote down their goals went on to earn considerably more when followed up years later.

Unfortunately, it appears neither study, despite being widely quoted, took place. I can't find any reference to them in academic journals, and I'm not the only one. Others have looked and, they too, have failed.

This said, there is research from Gail Matthews at the Dominican University of California, which does prove a similar point[3]. Professor Matthews took participants from a range of backgrounds, across a broad spectrum of age groups and nationalities. She assigned each of these participants to one of five groups:

- Group one wrote down their goals.

- Group two had goals but didn't write them down.

- Group three wrote down their goals and then made a commitment to action.

- Group four took this further by making their commitment to a friend.

- Group five went the furthest, writing their goal, making a commitment to a friend, and then providing progress reports to that friend.

Guess what happened when she revisited them at the end of four weeks? The participants who were providing progress reports to their friend achieved the greatest success. Those who made the commitment to a friend, but didn't provide a progress report, were second most successful; and the least successful were the people who didn't write their goals down.

Based on her findings, Professor Matthews pointed to a positive role both for writing down your goals and for establishing some accountability. You need someone to check in with and make sure you're doing what you said you'd do.

Given this importance of written goals, it's worth remembering what good goals look like. A goal, so the saying goes, is a dream with a plan. Without the plan, it will ever remain a dream, and dreams are prone to disappearing without trace.

If you create goals with no realistic prospect of success, you're doing yourself a massive disservice. That's where the SMART model of objective setting comes in. You've probably heard of the model before, but, in case you haven't, it's worth a quick overview.

SMART objectives are:

- **Specific** – "I want to be a better parent" is not a specific objective. It has no parameters and is likely to fail. What would make you a better parent? What is good enough? A more specific opening to an objective might be, "I want to make sure I spend at least one hour every evening wholly devoted to playing with my kids".

- **Measurable** – just as a goal needs to be specific, so you need to be able to measure the outcome to know if you've succeeded. "I want to get fit" is too vague. How would you measure it? "I want to be able to run 5k in under 25 minutes" is measurable – you either hit it or you don't.

- **Achievable** – a target which will stretch you is good, one you've no realistic prospect of hitting is not. You might like the idea of getting back to playing football but, if you're 45, it isn't too likely you're going to make it to the first team of a football league side. "I want to play a weekly five-a-side football match with my friends" is more achievable.

- **Relevant** – a goal is only meaningful if it's relevant to your life. Without this element, there really is no point in having the goal. Often, where a goal isn't relevant it's because it isn't really your goal. Remember the Pygmalion effect from chapter two? Many irrelevant goals are really based on other peoples' expectations of us, not on our own wishes. "I've got to qualify as an accountant" isn't a relevant goal if you really don't want to be an accountant.

- **Time-bound** – In some ways, this is the most important aspect of all. If you don't set a time-constraint, you'll never be held to the goal. However good that goal is, if you've left it open ended, you can still say it's 'on the go'. By setting deadlines, you're galvanizing action.

A truly SMART goal, then, might look like this:

"Over the next 30 days, I want to complete a daily gratitude diary, capturing three new things I'm grateful for each day".

- **Specific** – complete daily gratitude diary,

- **Measurable** – three new things each day,

- **Achievable** – this should take only a few minutes each day and requires no assistance,

- **Relevant** – it's a personal goal, aimed at achieving more gratitude, which has been shown to have positive mental health outcomes,

- **Time-bound** – for the next 30 days. You could even make this more specific by saying, starting on X date.

Thinking about your goals in the SMART structure will help you frame your objective and improve your chances of success. But there's still much more you can do...

Start small and build

There's an age-old dad joke which goes along the lines of:

- **Question**: How do you eat an elephant?

- **Answer**: One bite at a time.

Now, given my love of elephants, and for legal reasons, I should emphasise I'm not in favour of eating elephants under any circumstances. But, if you were presented with a situation where you HAD to eat an elephant, one bite at a time is certainly going to be a good strategy. Try to take on too much at once and you'll fail pretty quickly, and guess what? Your personal goals are just the same. Try to do too much all at once and nothing's going to work. Instead, you need to start small and work up to bigger successes (and there's some great psychology behind this).

American psychologist, Clark Leonard Hull discovered what he called the 'goal gradient effect'. We'll talk about goal gradients in a second, but it's worth pausing first to consider Hull himself. He was a fascinating guy, both because of his research, and because he embodied the notion of telling yourself better stories. When he was at college, he caught typhoid and nearly died. He was left with permanent amnesia and was told by many his academic career was over. He left college and became an apprentice mining engineer whereupon he promptly developed polio and was partially paralysed.

Most people, when confronted with such challenges, would have levelled down their expectations for the rest of their life. Had Hull operated from a fixed mindset, he could well have surrendered to learned helplessness and given up. Hull, however, was the epitome of a growth mindset. Instead of quitting, he found new academic pursuits and developed a love for psychology, going on to become Professor at Yale University and developing leading theories of motivation and behaviour – including goal gradient theory. Impressive, huh?

OK, so back to the story, what is goal gradient theory? Well, in simple terms it says the nearer you get to a goal, the more motivated you become to keep pushing to achieve it. The further away the goal seems, the harder it is to get yourself pumped up to take it on. If you've ever watched the end of a marathon, you'll see goal gradient theory played out in glorious technicolour. Twenty-five-and-a-bit miles into the marathon and runners look like they're hating life. They develop the 'marathon shuffle', just about managing to get one foot to move in front of the other. Then, they see the finish line gantry.

Suddenly their heads come up, their faces change, they find extra energy and they push on. The shuffle miraculously disappears, and they stride down the finishing chute looking like Roger Bannister in his prime. The simple proximity to the finish gives them access to a previously unavailable store of motivation and energy.

Marketers know all about goal gradients - they use them all the time. If you've ever got a loyalty card from a coffee shop and found they've given you two or three stamps to get you going, it's because they know you're more likely to keep using the card if you can see you've made progress. Likewise, when you buy something online and the little bar along the top shows you how close you are to completing the order, it's because you're less likely to drop out of the purchase if you can see you're nearly at the end. They're not daft, these marketing types.

"All very interesting", I hear you cry, "But how does this help me?" Well, I'm glad you asked. If you ask too much of yourself at once, you're likely to suffer from lower levels of motivation. Aiming straight for the 'big goal' will probably see you lose faith and drop out before you reach it. Instead, you need to break up the bigger objectives into a series of smaller waypoints. If you feel you're making progress toward the first step, you're more likely to keep going. Completing one step gives you motivation to get going on the second one, and so it goes on.

Case study 7.2 – The Professor

When I was a psychology undergraduate back in 1995, one of my classmates was struggling. She said she had too much work to do, and she'd reached the point of being overwhelmed. The mountain of reading, coursework, and essays was so much she was paralysed by inertia, so instead, she was sitting doing nothing.

One of our Professors listened to her complaint. He smiled, and then said something which has stuck with me for nearly 30 years. He said, "Just do something".

When you don't know where to start, you're on the wrong end of goal gradients. The distance from your goal seems so great, you can barely imagine a situation where you reach the goal. As a result, your motivation is at its lowest and you're prone to doing nothing.

The simple act of 'just doing something' was enough to help her break the pattern.

It's like a concept called Zorro circles, developed by Shawn Achor[4]. They're based on the legend of Zorro, in which the vigilante takes on an army by gradually building up an unbeatable skill. His mentor, Don Diego, initially trains him by putting a small circle in the sand. To start with, Zorro's required to remain in the circle at all times. Only when he mastered the first circle did Diego allow him to do more.

Why does this work? Well, research has shown people achieve more when they feel they're in control. When you work only on one aspect of your plan at a time, you not only benefit from the goal gradient, but also from greater feelings of control over your own destiny.

Create the environment

Another important aspect of achieving success is to consider the environment in which you work. Sometimes the way you set things up is helpful to achieving your goals, and sometimes it isn't.

One of the big changes many people have experienced over recent years is a move toward home working. Whilst this undoubtedly has its advantages, one of the disadvantages is a blurring of the lines between work and home. People no longer 'go to work' and then 'go home'. They work in the same place they relax – and often this means they aren't properly relaxing.

Creating a clear demarcation between working time and home time can be a valuable exercise. One of the changes I've made, for instance, is to stop using a laptop. Instead, I've bought a desktop computer which means if I want to work, I have to go to my office. When I leave for the night, I can't just send a few emails, or just write another couple of pages, unless I go back to the office and turn on the computer.

This idea of creating barriers is a powerful tool. You can make things easier for yourself by eliminating the things keeping you from doing what you want to do. You can also make it harder to do the things you want to stop doing by putting in place new barriers. Shawn Achor calls this the 'twenty-second rule'.

Imagine, for a second, you want to eat more healthily. You know you need to cut down on snacking, but every time you go to the kitchen for a cup of tea, you open the fridge to take out the milk, and there are all these wonderful, sweet treats staring out at you. However good your willpower, science tells us you're likely to crack – especially when you've had a busy day and you're tired.

What, then, if you took all the sweet treats and put them in a box? Then you put a padlock on the box, and you put the key for the padlock upstairs. You'd have to go upstairs, get the key, bring it down and open the box if you want to access the treat. The research indicates if this takes more than 20-seconds, you're unlikely to do it.

Likewise, if you are prone to scrolling endlessly through TikTok rather than doing your work, if you move TikTok to a folder on your phone and put a password on the folder which is so complex you have to open another document to copy and paste it, this whole process is likely to take more than 20 seconds. TikTok is then likely to sit there unloved – no more funny cat videos for you, Sandy.

You can also turn this on its head by making the 'good' activities easy to do. The most common example being exercise. Many people go to bed fully intending to get up in the morning and head to the gym. When morning comes around, their kit is still in the washing basket, their trainers are covered in mud from walking the dog, and their membership card is missing in action. The result? They have another coffee and think about eating a pastry instead.

By employing the same 20-second rule, you can get yourself ready the night before. Clean your trainers, pack your gym bag, get your membership card out. An even more powerful tip is to pack your 'coming home' clothes in your gym bag and lay out your exercise gear next to your bed. This way, when you get up you get straight into your gym gear, telling the brain this is happening, like it or not!

Do it now...

Gravel-voiced self-help legend Tony Robbins is fond of asking an important question of the people who come to see his shows. The question is, "When would 'now' be a good time to start?" In other words, why delay? Why isn't now the best time to get going?

One of the greatest enemies of success is delay. Too often you have clear ideas about what you want to achieve, and you know the date by which you'd like to achieve them, but you put off the 'doing' until some future date.

How many of the following statements resonate with you:

- I'm going to start my diet on Monday.

- As soon as we get back from holiday, I'm going to start looking for a new job.

- After Christmas is out of the way, I'm going to get fit.

- Once the kids have left home, we can start travelling a bit more.

Most of you will have fallen victim to at least one of these at some point – they're extremely common reactions to situations where you feel there's a difficult task ahead of you. Instead of starting to tackle the task, it gets kicked down the road to a future date. So, if you do this, you aren't alone. But it doesn't mean this is a good strategy for success, in fact quite the opposite is true. The longer you put off acting, the more embedded the idea of delay becomes, and the more likely you are to continue to dither. You're telling your brain the story that now isn't the right time to start – and it will respond in agreement.

The natural extension to 'not now' is an even more insidious trait of human beings – the 'when'. You tell yourself you'll be happy at some point in the future, but only 'when' a certain event happens. This comes in many forms:

- I'll be happy when I've lost the weight.

- I'll be happy when I've got a new job.

- I'll be happy when I'm fit.

- I'll be happy when we can start travelling more.

You can, no doubt, see the issue here. You tell yourself you'll be happy when a future event takes place, then you delay the event until some future point, thereby delaying your happiness. Doesn't sound like a good idea, does it? In fact, there are two things wrong with this scenario:

1. You're delaying things you could be doing now.

2. You're tying happiness to a future event, rather than giving yourself the possibility of being happy now.

How much better would it be to say:

- I'm going to start cutting back on my calories today and I'll be happy I'm taking matters in my own hands.

- I'm not happy in my current job so I'm going to look for a new one today. At least then I'll know my time here's limited and I can feel happy I'm moving towards a new job.

- I always feel happier when I've exercised, I'm going to go for a little walk/jog now. I'll start small but I know I'll feel much better for doing it.

- We love travel. It's tough with the kids, but I'm going to look at the possibility of a weekend away somewhere we've never been. I always get excited seeing new places.

These are only subtle shifts, but they're important for two reasons. Firstly, they create immediate action to drive you forward, however slowly, toward the bigger goals. Secondly, they break the link between a future event and happiness. Instead, you're giving yourself a reason to be happy now.

Research from Yale University[5] looked at the link between language and action. The specific research looked at savings behaviour and health decisions but has wider relevance to daily lives. It argued that because the English language distinguishes between a present and a future tense (it is raining today, it will rain tomorrow) it can be harder to relate to a future version of yourself than for people who speak languages which don't distinguish between tenses in the same way (it rains today, it rains tomorrow). This second group feel more connected to the future, it feels closer to them, and they take more action to protect the future version of themselves. They save more, exercise more, and eat better.

In my early career, when I was a financial adviser, I saw this play out with many clients. They saved less than they should for the future because they often saw the future version of themselves as being someone different. They rated their own needs as greater than the needs of this other person, rather than looking at the bigger picture of one person's current and future needs.

It's the climb

As Miley Cyrus is fond of telling us, 'There's always gonna be another mountain'. (Yes, I love a Miley tune, what of it?) If you spend all your time concentrating on the end goal, you are losing out on the greater part of the enjoyment. The climb itself is as much a part of the experience as reaching the summit. Both are parts of the whole. You shouldn't spend all your time concentrating on the end destination, instead you should take the time to enjoy the journey. My own example of climbing Kilimanjaro in chapter six demonstrates this point – without the enjoyment of the climb, the first visit would have been objectively disastrous. For me, though, it was one of the best experiences of my life.

Concentrating on enjoying the journey, the setbacks along the way, and the little wins in overcoming hurdles can make for a happy life, even if you don't end up where you thought you would. A walk is much more pleasant when you're mindful and take time to smell the flowers, even if you never get to the lake! It also gives you a chance to practice another Japanese technique –Kaizen.

Literally translated as 'improvement', Kaizen is a Japanese principle of continuous improvement, now employed by individuals and businesses around the world. The Team GB cycling team, under the leadership of David Brailsford employed Kaizen to become the dominant force in world cycling, always looking for the 'marginal gains', or small improvements, to achieve better performance. If you integrate Kaizen, alongside a principle of mindfully embracing the journey, you can look for the small areas of improvement every day. Consider this often-used example:

- If your current maximum output is 100 and you change nothing, at the end of the year, your output will be 100.

- If you can improve by just 1% each day, by the end of the year your output would be a whopping 3778.

- If, on the other hand, you go backwards by just 1% each day, you'd have an output of 2.6 at the one-year mark.

Seemingly small changes in either direction have massive long-term consequences on performance.

Don't go it alone

The final part of this picture is the power of others. Human beings are tribal creatures, and we work best when we're with other people, we don't do well alone. Once again, there are good evolutionary reasons why this should be the case. Think back to the time when our ancestors were hunter gatherers. They relied on the other members of their tribe to help them find food and shelter. If they were cast out from the tribe, they were heading towards almost certain death. No surprise, then, that we should develop a natural need to be around other people.

In possibly the most impressive analysis of humankind ever completed, the Harvard Study of Adult Development has been running for over 80 years. During this time, researchers have followed the same people (ultimately moving on to follow the original participants' children), with the aim of finding out what makes us happy. The findings of this study are set out by the current programme director, Robert Waldinger, in The Good Life[6]. Based on this study, you can sum up the single biggest contributor to happiness in just one word – connection. They found that the relationships in your life, and how happy you are in those relationships, have an incredibly powerful effect on your health. We all know that looking after our bodies is important. Now we also know that looking after our connections is perhaps equally so.

In the workplace, this has become more difficult in recent times, with the drive toward home working. Not only has this brought work into our home environment, but it's also reduced opportunities to build connections with the work 'tribe'. It's too early to tell what this will mean to the future of organisations, but it's something you can act on now to help maintain your social connections. Scheduling periodic in-person team meetings, arranging regular online 'catch-ups' or even just informal coffee mornings can all help maintain cohesion. Some organisations have introduced periods of 'co-working' where colleagues all work on their own projects whilst being dialled in to a Teams or Zoom call. The simple act of being in the (virtual) presence of your team can improve your outcomes.

One of my favourite pieces of research on the power of others comes from Simone Schnall[7]. In her study, she showed how our perception of challenge can be influenced by the support of others. The study was wonderfully simple. She asked participants to estimate the steepness of a hill. She found participants who were accompanied by someone they regarded as a friend estimated the hill to be less steep than those who were alone. In a follow up study, she further found participants estimated the hill to be less steep when they simply imagined a friend was with them. In other words, however difficult the challenges of life might be, they seem less severe when you're accompanied by people you trust.

As you saw from the Dominican University study (earlier in this chapter), having accountability to a friend can also make it more likely you'll achieve your goals. Meanwhile, solitary confinement is used as a form of punishment or even torture. Sold yet?

Now, before you go off and start calling up all the people you've ever known, a note of caution. Although it is good to be surrounded by people, you need them to be the right people. I told you this wasn't going to be a textbook and to prove the point, I'm going to quote the least expected source – reality TV star Vicky Pattison. When she appeared on the High Performance Podcast[8] (if you've not heard it, check it out, she was – I'll admit unexpectedly – brilliant), she talked about what I'll call the 'phone test'. Broadly, she said when your phone rings and you look at who's calling you, the person calling will fall into one of three groups:

- The people who instantly make you recoil – 'Oh, no, what do they want?' These are the ones who call you because they want something or because they want to moan about something in their life. These are 'draggers.'

- The people who 'don't set your world on fire' – they're pleasant enough and you might answer the phone, but it won't make your day. She calls these the 'middle of the roaders.'

- The final group are the ones whose name on the screen makes your heart beat a bit faster. The ones you can't wait to talk to. She calls this group the 'igniters.' You know they're ringing with something that will inspire you and help your own spark.

It might not be scientific, but it certainly works. When it comes to success, not all people in the 'tribe' are equal. Some people drag down your mood, they rain on your parade. Every idea you come up with is no good, wherever you want to go is going to be the wrong place, and invariably the topic of conversation is going to come round pretty quickly to their favourite subject – them. You're going on holiday to Tenerife, draggy-Maggie has just come back from Eleven-erife. You know the type.

These people are what Daniel Coyle describes[9] as 'bad apples'. The performance of teams can be massively influenced by just one or two people who bring negativity with them. These bad apples have the power to reduce overall group output. Human beings feed off each other. If someone brings enthusiasm to the table, you often describe it as being 'infectious' – because it is! Enthusiasm leads to enthusiasm. Igniters will ignite the entire team into more creativity, more excitement, and better results. On the other hand, 'draggers', or 'bad apples', have the potential to pull everyone down to their level of misery. If you want to achieve your goals, you need to guard against these people, both in work and in your social life.

I know it can be difficult to change your social circle and cutting loose old friends is tough, but as motivational speaker Jim Rohn apparently once said, "You are the average of the five people you spend the most time with". If you spend your time with draggers, you can expect to become one. If you spend your time with igniters, watch the sparks fly.

Perhaps my favourite approach to eliminating the draggers comes from the world-conquering New Zealand rugby union team – the All Blacks. Their mantra is simple and says it all: No Dick Heads.

Putting it into practice

Let's finish off with some concrete steps for performance improvement, building on the power of your new stories…

Exercise 7.1 - Define your why, and Ikigai

This takes some honesty but it's worth it. You need to ask yourself some important questions – the answers to which will help you discover your own Ikigai. For each, write as many things as come to mind:

a) What did I do on the best working day I've had? Pick a day when you left work thinking, "I'd have done that for nothing". What were you doing?

b) What do people come to me for? When someone says, "Can I pick your brains?" or "Can you help me with…" what are they talking about?

c) What really upsets you? This is important because it tells you about what you think the world needs. If you're upset about the lack of fitness in the general population, you've got a need – improved fitness.

d) What's the dream you've always had? When you've been in your quiet moments, when everything seemed possible, or when you think about retirement, what is it you really wanted to do with your life? Write down all those dreams – this is the yardstick against which any other possible Ikigai is to be measured.

e) What stops you? This will give you a feel for where the blockers might be. For most people, money is likely to fall into this group – but it doesn't need to. Doing what you love and finding a way to be paid for it is more achievable than you might think.

Finally, put these into an Ikigai Venn diagram to see where the overlaps occur. If you can't find all four overlapping – for example, you really can't make money from it – is there a way to make money in another way which would allow you to do the things you love, the world needs, and you're good at? Perhaps part-time?

Exercise 7.2 - Create your goals

Take some time to write out your goals. Think about the things you want to accomplish and write them in the SMART format. Don't just take the big picture goal, though. Think about the smaller sub-goals you'll need to hit on the way. This is crucial. Remember, if you only focus on the big goal, it can be daunting. You need to think about the smaller goals, the Zorro circles you'll need to hit, along the way.

By having these smaller goals, you can benefit from the 'goal gradient' as you push closer to achieving them.

Exercise 7.3 - Take action now on the first steps

This is so important. Do not, I repeat, do not put off the start until tomorrow. Make the first step something you can do right now. However small a step that might be, just getting on the way will pay long-term dividends.

Exercise 7.4 - Smell the flowers

Make a point each day to take some time to appreciate the world around you. Whether this means taking a walk around your local area, sitting in the garden with a coffee, or even just the gratitude journalling from chapter six. Make the journey a goal in its own right.

You only get one crack at life. The Stoic philosophers used to say, 'Memento Mori', which translates as 'remember you are dying'. Not a pleasant thought, but an important one. Every minute gone by is a moment that isn't coming back. The only moment of your life which is guaranteed is the one you're living right now. Make the most of it.

Exercise 7.5 - Pick (and prune) your team

OK, so this is the last exercise I'm going to set you and it's both the most difficult, and the most valuable, in my opinion. I want you to consider the people in your life at the moment through the lens of the 'phone test'.

Which of them are the 'igniters', the ones who you can't wait to speak to? When the phone rings, whose name would make you snatch up the phone? On the other hand, who are your 'draggers'? Who makes you think seriously about letting voicemail do the heavy lifting?

If it's true that you're the average of the five people you spend the most time with, how much time are you spending with those draggers, and is this making you a dragger too? If so, perhaps now is the time to start thinking about making some changes.

Sometimes, to move forwards you need to phase out the bad apples. If someone isn't helping to make your life better, perhaps spending a bit less time with them and more time with the igniters in your life, might help you to feel more positive.

"Too long; didn't read" chapter summary

If you know what you want, your brain's more likely to look for opportunities to help you achieve your goals. If you don't know what good looks like, your internal filters are likely to automatically walk past opportunities which could have changed your life.

A starting point is to define your 'Why'. The 'Why' is the bigger purpose than you, the thing getting you up in the morning – the reason to keep pushing on when things feel tough.

The Japanese have a principle of 'Ikigai'. They say ultimate happiness and satisfaction comes from doing things which meet four key principles:

- You're good at it,

- The world needs it,

- You enjoy it,

- You can earn money from it.

Once you know your purpose, you need to define and implement good goals. The age-old model for goal setting – SMART – still holds true. Goals need to be specific, measurable, achievable, relevant, and timebound.

You should start with smaller goals. The quick wins. These will give you the positivity to keep pushing on. Starting with too big a goal is likely to lead to loss of motivation when you don't feel you're making progress.

Your environment plays a factor in your success. You should make it as easy as possible to do the right things and make it harder for you to do the wrong things. The things you want to do should never be more than 20-seconds away and the things you don't, or want to move away from, should always be more than that.

Now is the best time to get going and you should make sure you enjoy the journey rather than just focusing on the destination. The walk up the mountain can be as enjoyable as the view from the top.

Don't go it alone. You're a tribal creature – you're hard wired to be with other people. It isn't just coincidence that solitary confinement is used as a form of punishment. Surround yourself with people who make you feel good about yourself.

FINAL THOUGHTS

THE HUMAN BRAIN is a complex and wonderful thing. Everything ever made by humankind is the product of the brain. It has allowed us to do enormous good – from medicine that prolongs life, through to technology allowing us to connect to any other person on the planet in seconds. At our fingertips through the internet is the collected wisdom of the ages, and all made possible by the brain.

Unfortunately, just as it has done tremendous good, so the brain has done immeasurable harm. Weapons, murder, and chaos all stem from the same brains in our heads.

Closer to home, your own brain can inspire you to explore the world, to create, to embrace opportunity and to live life to the fullest. Alternatively, it can hold you back, convince you you're worthless, and imprison you in a seemingly impenetrable fortress of despair. The difference between these two outcomes, for many people, is no more than the stories the brain has been given to believe.

For such a complex thing, the brain will believe nonsense if you tell it to. It'll accept your worst fears as fact, it'll make life-or-death decisions based on minimal information, and it'll cling with a steely resolve to the beliefs you've told it to hold. So, you need to make sure you're giving it the right beliefs.

You have the potential to live a happier and more fulfilled life. The secret to achieving that life lies in the way you use your brain, and the stories you tell it to believe.

In this book you've seen how people become bogged down with learned helplessness, how the absence of hope and negative expectations can diminish quality of life. But you've also seen the other side – how creating more positive expectations can shift your perception and lead to greater success. How expecting more from yourself and others can become a self-fulfilling prophecy. You've seen the power of story and how creating better filters results in greater happiness, and you've even looked at ways to overcome our evolutionary bias toward negativity. You, yes you, have the potential to be more lion and less rabbit.

By cultivating a more open and 'growth' based mindset, you can develop more optimism in life which, as Martin Seligman and others have shown, can improve both physical and mental health. And, of course, you've looked at the power of gratitude and mindfulness – calming the mind and appreciating the good things you've already got. The benefits there are vast.

What happens from here is in your hands. We know from experience people will fall into three broad groups. One group will take this information and do absolutely nothing with it. It'll be a case of here today, gone tomorrow. A second group will take on board some of what they've read and go through a few of the exercises. This group will achieve some benefits both now and in the longer term.

Then there's the third group - this is the group I'm excited for and the group I want you to be in. This group will do what I did all those years ago. They'll take on board what they've read and use it as a springboard for the rest of their lives.

It is easy to 'over egg the pudding', but the information contained in these pages has been transformational for me and I believe it can be for you. If you're not living the life you want to lead, you have the power to make changes. It isn't easy and it isn't instant, but it is worth it. We all have the power to be happy, why wouldn't you try your best to seize it.

Let me leave you with one final incentive from the work of Shawn Achor, who turns conventionally accepted wisdom on its head. Many people believe they'll be happy when they're successful. You've already read about this scourge of 'when' as something to hold you back – 'I'll be happy when...', but there's something else, something I've kept back.

What Shawn Achor showed is that we're wrong to think success will lead to happiness. What the research shows is, instead, happiness leads to success. If you focus on what will be in the future, you're limiting yourself. Instead, if you can change your lens and find your way to being happy now, if you approach the world with optimism and positivity, you see opportunities everywhere, and you're more likely to take them. Being happy right now makes you more likely to be successful in the future!

Some of the things you've looked at in these pages will require you to make changes – and some of them are big. But don't be daunted by that. You make massive changes all the time, even if you don't realise it. You leave school, start a job, change jobs, move house, start a relationship (maybe you end one). You rent, buy or sell houses. You may even have kids. All these changes are huge. Don't doubt your ability to make change. If you want to live a happier and more fulfilled life, you can. Commit and act, the rest will fall into place.

I'd love you to join our community. I'm so excited to hear your good news stories and the ways you've been able to rewrite your own stories. Get in touch through our website (www.aboutpeakperformance.co.uk/rewritten), sign up for our newsletter, or just say, 'Hi'. I'd love to hear about your journey, I really would.

In the meantime, I wish you every success as you grow towards greater happiness. You deserve it.

ACKNOWLEDGEMENTS

I've had a lot of help from some wonderful people in getting this book out there. Big thanks to Katie for keeping me on the right path and making some inspired changes – I'm looking forward to the next project.

Thanks to Phil for the nudge to get this done, it was just what I needed.

I had the help of some fabulous trial readers, thanks to Sandy, Jason, Steve, Dan, and Rob for all agreeing to be guinea pigs. I really appreciate it.

My illustrator, Nastja and cover designer Ajibola both hit the brief just as I'd hoped.

Finally, the biggest thanks as always to Madeline and my three boys for making it all worthwhile. Love you all.

REFERENCES:

Chapter one

1. Seligman ME (1972). "Learned helplessness". Annual Review of Medicine. 23 (1): 407–412. doi:10.1146/annurev.me.23.020172.002203. PMID 4566487.

2. Learned Optimism (1991) Martin Seligman – Nicholas Brealey Publishing

Chapter two

1. Richter, C. P. (1957). "On the phenomenon of sudden death in animals and man." American Journal of Physiology, 189(2), 609-617.

2. Snyder, C (2003) The psychology of hope: You can get here from there. Free Press. ISBN 0743254449

3. Gilman, R., Schumm, J. A., & Chard, K. M. (2012). "Hope as a change mechanism in the treatment of posttraumatic stress disorder". Psychological Trauma: Theory, Research, Practice, and Policy, 4(3), 270–277.

4. Kristof, N (2015) "The Power of Hope is Real". New York Times (Online) https://www.nytimes.com/2015/05/21/opinion/nicholas-kristof-the-power-of-hope-is-real.html

5. Robson, David (2022) "The Expectation Effect". Cannongate Books

6. Charlesworth JE, Petkovic G, Kelley JM, Hunter M, Onakpoya I, Roberts N, Miller FG, Howick J (2017). "Effects of placebos without deception compared with no treatment: A systematic review and meta-analysis". Journal of Evidence-Based Medicine (Systematic review and meta-analysis). 10 (2): 97–107.

7. Kirsch I (1985). "Response expectancy as a determinant of experience and behavior". American Psychologist. 40 (11): 1189–1202.

8. Miller, Franklin G. (2003). "Sham Surgery: An Ethical Analysis". The American Journal of Bioethics. 3 (4): 41–48.

9. Häuser, Winfried; Hansen, Ernil; Enck, Paul (2012). "Nocebo Phenomena in Medicine". Deutsches Ärzteblatt. (Online) 109 (26): 459–465.

10. Haas, Julia W.; Bender, Friederike L.; Ballou, Sarah; Kelley, John M.; Wilhelm, Marcel; Miller, Franklin G.; Rief, Winfried; Kaptchuk, Ted J. (2022). "Frequency of Adverse Events in the Placebo Arms of COVID-19 Vaccine Trials:

A Systematic Review and Meta-analysis". (Online) JAMA Netw Open. 2022;5(1):e2143955. doi:10.1001/jamanetworkopen.2021.43955

11. Rosenthal. R. and Jacobson, L. (1968). "Pygmalion in the classroom". The Urban Review. 3 (1): 16–20.

12. Banayan, Alex (2018) "The Third Door: The Wild Quest to Uncover How the World's Most Successful People Launched Their Careers". Currency

13. Robbins, Mel (2023) "The High 5 Habit". Hay House

14. Pink, Daniel (2019) "When: The Scientific secrets of Perfect Timing". Canongate Books

Chapter three

1. Heim, S. and Keil, A (2017) Too much information, too little time: How the brain separates important from unimportant things in our fast-paced media world (online) https://bit.ly/heimkeil

2. HR News (2022) Social Media: People can scroll the length of Mount Everest in 20 days! https://bit.ly/scrolleverest

3. Peters, Steve (2012) "The Chimp Paradox: The Mind Management Programme for Confidence, Success and Happiness". Vermillion.

4. Twin Cities (1994) "Sunday Bulletin Board: `I have dubbed it The Baader-Meinhof Phenomenon'". (Online) https://www.twincities.com/1994/10/16/baader-meinhof-phenomenon-sunday-bulletin-board/

5. Zwicky, Arnold (2005). "Language Log: Just between Dr. Language and I". itre.cis.upenn.edu. Retrieved 2023-03-28.

6. Content Marketing Institute (2018) "Storytelling with Joe Lazauskas" (Online) https://bit.ly/3Z0ovQX

7. Wade, K.A., Garry, M., Don Read, J. et al. (2002) "A picture is worth a thousand lies: Using false photographs to create false childhood memories". Psychonomic Bulletin & Review 9, 597–603.

8. Frankl, Viktor (1946) "Man's search for meaning". English version Beacon Press

9. Gawdat, Mo (2022) "That Little Voice in Your Head". Bluebird

10. Achor, Shawn (2018) "Big Potential". Virgin books

11. Whitten, Helen (2009) "Cognitive Behavioural Coaching Techniques for Dummies". For Dummies

References:

Chapter four

1. Tseng, J. and Poppenk, J. (2020) "Brain meta-state transitions demarcate thoughts across contexts exposing the mental noise of trait neuroticism". Nature Communications, v11, Article 3480 (online) https://bit.ly/3Z1wCN8

2. Peters, S (2012) "The Chimp Paradox: The Mind Management Programme for Confidence, Success and Happiness". Vermillion.

3. Hankel, Isiah (2014) "Black Hole Focus". Capstone

4. Achor, Shawn (2011) "The Happiness Advantage". Virgin Books

Chapter five

1. Dweck, Carol (2012) "Mindset: How You Can Fulfil You Potential". Robinson

2. Seligman, Martin (1991) "Learned Optimism". Nicholas Brealey Publishing

3. Maguire, E. et al (2000) "Navigation related structural change in the hippocampi of taxi drivers. Proceedings of the National Academy of Sciences". USA, 97(8) pp 4398-4403

4. Tao W, Zhao D, Yue H, Horton I, Tian X, Xu Z and Sun H-J (2022) "The Influence of Growth Mindset on the Mental

Health and Life Events of College Students". Front. Psychol. 13:821206. doi: 10.3389/fpsyg.2022.821206

5. Boehm, J. K., Peterson, C., Kivimaki, M., & Kubzansky, L. (2011). "A prospective study of positive psychological well-being and coronary heart disease". Health Psychology, 30(3), 259–267.

6. Amonoo, HL. Celano, CM. Sadlonova, M. Huffman, JC. (2021) "Is Optimism a Protective Factor for Cardiovascular Disease?" Curr Cardiol Rep. 2021 Oct 1;23(11):158.

7. Noskeau, Rebecca et al (2021) "Connecting the Dots Between Mindset and Imposter Phenomenon, via Fear of Failure and Goal Orientation, in Working Adults. Frontiers in Psychology". 12:588438. doi: 10.3389/fpsyg.2021.588438

Chapter six

1. Van Cuylenburg, Hugh (2019) "The Resilience Project: Finding Happiness Through Gratitude Empathy and Mindfulness". Ebury Australia.

2. Seligman, Martin et al, (2005) "Positive psychology progress: Empirical Validation of Interventions". American Psychologist, v60, no 5, pp 410-421

3. Kini, Prathik et al (2015) "The effects of gratitude expression on neural activity". Neuroimage, v128, pp 1-10.

4. Millstein, Rachel et al (2016) "The Effects of optimism and gratitude on adherence, functioning and mental health following and acute coronary syndrome. General Hospital Psychiatry", 43, pp 17-22

5. Shakerifard M, et al. (2019) "Effect of Gratitude on Mental Health with Mediating Role of Positive and Negative Affect". Iran Journal of Education and Community Health. 2019;6 (2):87-93.

6. Kyeong, Sunghyon (2017) "Effects of gratitude meditation on neural network functional connectivity and brain-heart coupling". Scientific Reports 7:5058

7. Shaprio, Shauna (2009) "The Integration of Mindfulness and Psychology", Clin Pyschol 65: 555-560

8. Tolle, Eckhart (1999) "The Power of Now: A Guide to Spiritual Enlightenment", New World Library.

Chapter seven

1. Sinek, Simon (2011) "Start With Why". Penguin

2. Garcia, Hector and Miralles, Francesc (2017)" Ikigai". Hutchinson

3. Matthews, Gail (2007) "Written Goal Study Dominican University" (online) https://bit.ly/3sHVI7i

4. Achor, Shawn (2011) "The Happiness Advantage". Virgin Books

5. Chen, Keith (2013) "The language we speak predicts saving and health behaviour" (Online) https://bit.ly/3R01wTW

6. Waldinger, Robert and Shulz, Marc (2023) "The Good Life and How to Live it: Lessons from the World's Longest Study on Happiness". Rider

7. Schnall S, Harber KD, Stefanucci JK, Proffitt DR. (2008) "Social Support and the Perception of Geographical Slant". J Exp Soc Psychol. 2008 Sep 1;44(5):1246-1255.

8. High Performance Podcast (2022) "Vicky Pattison: Listen without prejudice" https://www.thehighperformancepodcast.com/podcast/vickypattison

9. Coyle, Daniel (2019) "The Culture Code: The Secrets of Highly Successful Groups". Random House Business

t

Printed in Great Britain
by Amazon

31236184R00112